Nancy Vale's Knitwear

NANCY VALE'S KNITWEAR

NANCY VALE

BALLANTINE BOOKS ■ NEW YORK

Portions of this text originally appeared in *Knitwear: Designer Handknits by Nancy Vale.*

Photography and illustration credits can be found at the back of the book.

Library of Congress Cataloging-in-Publication Data

Vale, Nancy, 1924–
  Nancy Vale's knitwear.

  1. Sweaters.   2. Knitting—Patterns.   I. Title.
II. Title: Knitwear.
TT825.V35   1987   746.9′2   86-48000
ISBN: 0-345-33039-0

Interior design by Michaelis/Carpelis Design Assoc., Inc.

Filmset by TGA Communications, New York

Printed and bound in Japan by Dai Nippon Printing Co.

First Edition: October 1987
10 9 8 7 6 5 4 3 2 1

CONTENTS

INTRODUCTION

Welcome to *Nancy Vale's Knitwear*. This book offers an exciting new look at the art of handknitting. Irresistible to anyone who appreciates beautiful handwork, it features exclusive patterns that I have created for couture houses and designer collections all over the world.

Nancy Vale's Knitwear grew out of my business in handknitwear. In the last fourteen years, I have progressed from knitting coats and sweaters for my children to designing and supplying high fashion knitwear for the likes of Ralph Lauren and Calvin Klein.

It all started after I'd set five children firmly on their feet in the world and was looking for a new challenge. I'd been a fanatical knitter all my life so I thought I'd try going professional, making handknits for export. I knitted up some baby wear, introduced myself to some of the London buying houses and from then, haven't looked back. Over the years, I've been encouraged to design children's wear, then accessories, and finally fashion wear, which I have now been designing for ten years.

It is a real English cottage industry. I started with some 200 knitters working in their own homes; today, I have well over a thousand knitters. I have a center near my home in Kent, and from there the patterns and yarn are taken out to group leaders who distribute them to, and later collect the finished work from, their group of knitters. The garments are then returned to the center where they are checked, labelled, pressed, and packed. For a long time I traveled up and down

INTRODUCTION

to London with my great big suitcases to sell my garments, but now the designers themselves or buyers from the most grandiose and exclusive stores all over the world prefer to come to see me, amidst hundreds of sweaters. They love to see my ever-increasing pile of handknits for which I have such enormous enthusiasm. I share a great rapport with these buyers, who really appreciate the unique quality of handknitting.

I have had the good fortune and privilege of working closely with Ralph Lauren over many years, as well as with Calvin Klein and Gloria Sachs, and such distinguished stores as Bergdorf Goodman, Neiman Marcus, Saks Fifth Avenue, Bloomingdales, Paul Stuart, Henri Bendel, Mark Cross, Burberry's U.S.A., Abercrombie and Fitch, Marshall Field, and Harold's of Texas. I never run short of ideas; in fact they tumble out of my head faster than I can design them.

I know that handknits sold by the famous names in fashion are only within reach of the wealthy. But I have always wanted to make them available to handknitters everywhere.

First I published some of my designs in magazine form in England. Ballantine Books discovered them and suggested putting a really lovely book together. I am very glad indeed of

this chance to share with you some of my most distinctive designs. Now you can have the pleasure of creating these garments for yourself, family, and friends.

All are made in yarns easily found in the shops. I do not specify particular brands of yarn because I feel it is important that you buy whichever yarn is most easily available to you. The brand in fact should make no difference as long as the equivalent weight is used and the gauge followed. This makes the garments affordable as well as collectible; something to wear with confidence now, and to keep forever.

I hope you find *Nancy Vale's Knitwear* as exciting as I do. I am sure this will be the start of a series of books that will let you keep up with the best in international high fashion knitting.

Happy knitting!

ABBREVIATIONS

beg	begin(ning)
CC	contrasting color
cm	centimeter(s)
cont	continu(e)(ing)
dec	decreas(e)(ing)
foll	follow(s)(ing)
gm	gram(s)
inc	increas(e)(ing)
k	knit
M	make one
mm	millimeter(s)
MC	main color
p	purl
psso	pass slip stitch over
rem	remain(s)(ing)
rep	repeat
sl	slip
st(s)	stitch(es)
st st	stockinette stitch
tbl	through the back loop(s)
tog	together
yo	yarn over (hook or needle)

Nancy Vale's Knitwear

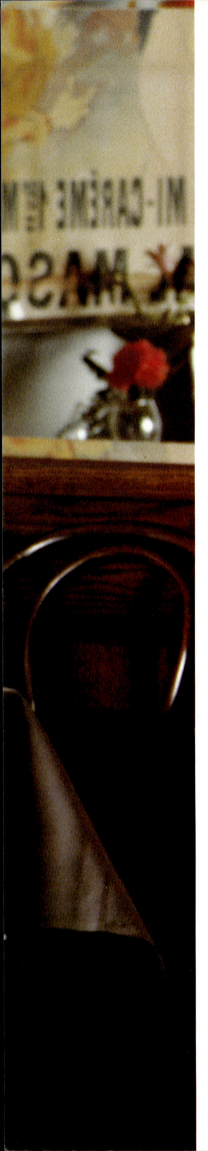

Timeless Classics

Timeless Classics that people love to wear are what I aim for when I design my handknits—garments so classical and beautiful that people will be able to wear them with pleasure and confidence year in and year out. Very rarely does one tire of a piece of clothing that manages to combine beauty and comfort, and it gives intense satisfaction to the knitter to see the finished garment. ■ Knitting is indeed a work of art—it can be as delicate and intricate as fine lace, as rich and colorful as a painting, and as exciting as the latest and most impressionable fashionwear. I chose the garments in this first section for their classical and enduring simplicity.

SLANT SPECIAL

A delightfully feminine cardigan with its slant stitch and ripple bind-off at the neck. Made on fairly large needles, it is very light, soft and easy to knit.

Sizes:
To fit 34 (36)"/86 (91)cm and 38 (40)"/96(102)cm. Directions are for the smaller size with the larger size in parentheses.

Materials:
9 50 gm balls sportweight wool
8 buttons

Needles:
One pair each size 3 (3.25mm) and size 7 (5mm) knitting needles or size needed to obtain gauge.

Gauge:
21 sts = 4" (10cm) on #7 (5mm) needles over pattern.

Back:
With smaller needles cast on 95 (107) sts and work in k1, p1 rib for 3½" (9cm). Change to larger needles and pattern as follows:

Row 1: Sl 1, (p3, k3) 7(8) times, p3, k3, p3, (k3, p3) 7 (8) times, k1 tbl.
Row 2: Sl 1, k3 (p3, k3) 7(8) times, p3, (k3, p3) 7 (8) times, k3, k1 tbl.
Row 3: Sl 1, p2 (k3, p3) 7(8) times, k5, (p3, k3) 7 (8) times, p2, k1 tbl.
Row 4: Sl 1, k2 (p3, k3) 7(8) times, p5, (k3, p3) 7 (8) times, k2, k1 tbl.
Row 5: Sl 1, p1 (k3, p3) 7(8) times, k3, p1, k3, (p3, k3) 7 (8) times, p1, k1 tbl.
Row 6: Sl 1, k1 (p3, k3) 7(8) times, p3, k1, p3, (k3, p3) 7 (8) times, k1, k1 tbl.
Row 7: Sl 1, (k3, p3) 7(8) times, k3, p3, k3, (p3, k3) 7 (8) times, k1 tbl.
Row 8: Sl 1, (p3, k3) 7(8) times, p3, k3, p3, (k3, p3) 7(8) times, k1 tbl.
Row 9: Sl 1, k2 (p3, k3) 7(8) times, p5, (k3, p3) 7 (8) times, k2, k1 tbl.
Row 10: Sl 1, p2 (k3, p3) 7(8) times, k5, (p3, k3) 7 (8) times, p2, k1 tbl.
Row 11: Sl 1, k1 (p3, k3) 7(8) times, p3, k1, p3, (k3, p3) 7 (8) times, k1, k1 tbl.
Row 12: Sl 1, p1, (k3, p3) 7(8) times, k3, p1, k3, (p3, k3) 7 (8) times, p1, k1 tbl.

These 12 rows form the pattern which is repeated throughout. Work evenly until piece measures 15" (38cm), or desired length to underarm, from beg. End with right side facing.

Shape Armholes:
Keeping pattern correct, bind off 3 sts at beg of next 2 rows. K2tog each side of every row until 75 (83) sts rem. Cont in pattern until piece measures 2½" (6cm) from armhole bind off. Now work in k1, p1 rib until armhole measures 8" (20cm) from armhole bind off. End with right side facing.

Shape Shoulders:
Bind off 12 (14) sts at beg of next 4 rows. Place rem sts on holder for neck.

Right Front:
With smaller needles cast on 49 (55) sts and work in k1, p1 rib with garter st border as follows:

Row 1: Sl 1, k8, rib to end.
Row 2: Sl 1, rib to last 9 sts, k8, k1 tbl.
Row 3: (make buttonhole) Sl 1, k2, yo, k2tog, k4, rib to end.

Repeat rows 1 and 2 until rib measures 3½" (9cm), *at the same time* make another buttonhole 2½" (6cm) after the first one. End with right side facing. Change to larger needles and work in pattern as follows, making buttonholes every 2½" (6cm) (the last buttonhole will come in neckband):

Row 1: Sl 1, k8, p1 *k3, p3 repeat from * to last 3 sts, k2, k1 tbl.
Row 2: Sl 1, p2 *k3, p3 repeat from * to last 10 sts, k9, k1 tbl.
Row 3: Sl 1, k8, p2 *k3, p3 repeat from * to last 2 sts, k1, k1 tbl.
Row 4: Sl 1, p1 *k3, p3 repeat from * to last 11 sts, k10, k1 tbl.
Row 5: Sl 1, k8, *p3, k3 repeat from * to last 4 sts, p3, k1 tbl.

SLANT SPECIAL

Row 6: Sl 1, *k3, p3 repeat from * to last 12 sts, k11, k1 tbl.
Row 7: Sl 1, k9, *p3, k3 repeat from * to last 3 sts, p2, k1 tbl.
Row 8: Sl 1, k2, *p3, k3 repeat from * to last 10 sts, p1, k8, k1 tbl.
Row 9: Sl 1, k10, *p3, k3 repeat from * to last 2 sts, p1, k1 tbl.
Row 10: Sl 1, k1, *p3, k3 repeat from * to last 11 sts, p2, k8, k1 tbl.
Row 11: Sl 1, k8, *k3, p3 repeat from * to last 4 sts, k3, k1 tbl.
Row 12: Sl 1, *p3, k3 repeat from * to last 12 sts, p3 k8, k1 tbl.

Cont to work in pattern until piece measures same as back to underarm. End at armhole edge.

Shape Armhole:
Bind off 3 sts at the beg of the next row. Then dec 1 st at side edge every row until 41 (45) sts rem. Work evenly until same length as back to rib. Keeping the 9 st garter border, work in k1, p1 rib. When 3″ (7.5cm) of ribbing has been worked, finish at neck edge. Place last 10 (12) sts onto holder to pick up for neck.

Shape Neck:
Dec 1 st at neck edge every other row until 24 (28) sts rem. End at side edge.

Shape Shoulders:
Bind off 12 (14) sts at beg of next row. Work 1 row. Bind off 12 (14) sts at beg of next row.

Left Front:
Work as for right front, slanting the rib the opposite way, reversing all shaping, and omitting buttonholes.

Sleeves:
With smaller needles cast on 42 sts and work in k1, p1 rib for 3½″ (9cm). Inc into every st but one across last row, 83 sts. Change to larger needles and work in pattern as for back. (Work the bracketed (k3, p3) or (p3, k3) 6 times instead of 7 or 8). Work evenly until sleeve measures 18″ (46cm), or desired length to underarm, from beg.

Shape Cap:
Bind off 4 sts at beg of next 2 rows. Dec 1 st at each end every row until 51 sts rem. Then dec 1 st each side every other row until 31 sts rem. End with wrong side facing. Bind off in k working 2 sts tog all along row.

Neckband:
Join shoulder seams. With smaller needles, right side facing beg at right front and pick up 10 (12) sts from center, 23 sts up right side, 27 sts from back, 23 sts down left side and 10 (12) sts from left center. Work 3 rows in garter st. Make buttonhole at beg of next row. K 2 rows. Bind off in ripple edge as follows:
Bind off 2 sts, *sl st onto left hand needle, bind on 2 sts, bind off 4 sts. Repeat from * to end.

Finishing:
Pin sleeves into armholes and sew into place. Sew side and sleeve seams. Sew on buttons.

IN THE NAVY

Fresh and charming, this pattern is very popular. It is knit in a simple slip stitch tweed pattern which works well with the flattering sailor collar. Made in fingering weight cotton, it is comfortably cool and light, and you can wear it with trousers, skirts or shorts.

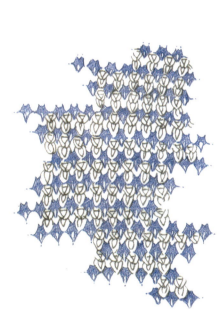

Sizes:
To fit 34 (36, 38, 40)"/ 86 (91, 96, 102)cm bust. Directions are for small size with larger sizes in parentheses.

Materials
5 (5, 6, 6) 50 gram balls of fingering weight cotton in MC (navy)
4 (4, 5, 5) 50 gram balls of fingering weight cotton in CC (white)

Needles:
One pair each sizes 2 (3mm) and 3 (3.25mm) knitting needles or size needed to obtain gauge.

Gauge:
25 sts and 40 rows = 4" (10cm) on #3 needles over slip-stitch tweed pattern.

Back:
With smaller needles and MC, cast on 109 (115, 121, 127) sts and work in k1, p1 rib for 1" (2.5cm). Change to larger needles and work in slip-stitch tweed pattern as follows:

Row 1: (wrong side facing) With MC k 1 yfwd (yarn forward over needle),* Sl 1 purlwise with yarn still in front, k1, rep from * to end.
Row 2: With CC k1, * ktog the 2 crossed sts, p1, rep from * to end.
Row 3: With CC k1, * k1 yfwd, sl 1 purlwise with yarn still in front, rep from * end k2.
Row 4: With MC k1, * p1, knit tog with 2 crossed sts, rep from * end p1, k1.

These 4 rows form pattern. Cont to work in pattern until piece measures 14½ (14½, 15, 15)"/ 37 (37, 38, 38)cms from beg. End with right side facing.

Shape Armholes:
(NOTE: When binding off, knit the 2 crossed sts tog and count as 1 st.) Bind off 4 sts at the beg of the next 2 rows, then dec 1 st at each end every other row until 93 (99, 105, 111) sts rem. Cont in pattern until piece measures 23 (23, 23½, 23½)"/ 58.5 (58.5, 60, 60)cms from beg. End with right side facing.

Shape Shoulders:
Bind off 14 (15, 16, 17) sts at beg of next 4 rows. Bind off rem 37 (39, 41, 43) sts.

Front:
Work as for back until armhole shaping is completed. End with right side facing.

Shape Neck:
Pattern across 46 (49, 52, 55) sts. Turn and work 1 side only. Dec 1 st at neck edge on next row and then every 4th row until 28 (30, 32, 34) sts rem. Work evenly in pattern until piece measures same as back to shoulder shaping. End with right side facing.

Shape Shoulder:
Bind off 14 (15, 16, 17) sts at beg of next row. Work one row. Repeat bind off on shoulder edge. Join yarn to 2nd side and bind off 1 st at neck edge. Work to correspond to first side, reversing all shaping.

Sleeves:
With smaller needles and MC cast on 75 (77, 79, 81) sts and work in k1,p1 rib for 1" (2.5cm). Inc.20 sts evenly across last row, 95 (97, 99, 101) sts. Change to larger needles and work in pattern until sleeve measures 5" (13cm) from beg. End with right side facing.

Shape Cap:
Bind off 4 sts at beg of next 2 rows, then dec 1 st at each end of every row until 25 (27, 27, 29) sts rem. Bind off rem sts (knit st on a wrong side row).

Collar:
With smaller needles and MC (or CC if preferred) cast on 90 (92, 94, 96) sts. Change to larger needles and work 11 rows in garter st. Next row: k6, p 78 (80, 82, 84), k6. Next row: Knit. Rep these two rows until piece measures 8" (20cm) from beg. End with a purl row. Next row: k28 and turn. Working one side only, cont in st st with garter st border and k2tog at neck edge every 4th row until 8 sts rem. Mark this row. Work in garter st until piece measures 12" (30cm) from marked row. Bind off. Join yarn to other side and bind off 34 (36, 38, 40) sts. Work to end of row. Complete to match first side, reversing all shaping.

Finishing:
Sew shoulder seams. Sew collar into place, leaving the ties for bow free. Sew in sleeves. Sew side and sleeve seams.

CABLE NEWS

However fashions may come and go, cables remain one of handknitting's most effective and beautiful stitches. This slipover vest with a simple cable combined with a twist stitch will keep its shape forever and its tremendous elasticity means it will fit most sizes perfectly. Wonderful for both men and women.

Sizes:
This stitch is elastic in quality. To fit 38(40)"/ 96 (102)cm. Directions are for the smaller size with the larger size in parentheses.

Materials:
9 50 gram balls of sportweight Shetland wool

Needles:
One pair each, sizes 3 (3.25mm) and 5 (4mm) knitting needles or size needed to obtain gauge.

Gauge:
10 sts = 2" (5cm) on #5 (4mm) needles over st st.

Abbreviations:
RT = Right twist = k2tog, leave sts on left needle, k 1st st again, then sl both sts from needle tog.
C3 = Cable 3 = sl next 3 sts onto a cable needle and leave in front of work, k 3, then k 3 sts from cable needle.

Back:
With smaller needles, cast on 97 (104) sts and work in k1, p1 rib and twist as follows:

Row 1: Sl 1, p1, * RT, p1, k1, p1, k1, p1. Rep from * to last 4 sts, RT, p1, k1 tbl.
Row 2: Sl 1, k1, p2, * k1, p1, k1, p1, k1, p2. Rep from * to last 2 sts, end k1, k1 tbl.
Repeat these 2 rows until piece measures 2¾" (7cm) from beg. End with wrong side facing. Inc in the next row as follows: Sl 1, (k1, p1) into next st, p2 * (k1, p1) into next 5 sts, p2. Rep from * to last 2 sts, (k1, p1) into next st, k1 tbl, 164 (176) sts. Change to larger needles and work in pattern as follows:

Row 1: Sl 1, p2, * RT, p2, k6, p2. Rep from * to last 5 sts, RT, p2, k1 tbl.
Row 2: Sl 1, k2, p2, * k2, p6, k2, p2. Rep from * to last 3 sts, k2, k1 tbl.
Row 3: Sl 1, p2, * RT, p2, C3, p2. Rep from * to last 5 sts, RT, p2, k1 tbl.

Cont working row 1 for all right side rows and row 2 for all wrong side rows. Row 3 is repeated every 10th row. Work evenly in this pattern until back measures 16½" (42cm) from beg.

Shape Armholes:
Bind off 6 sts at beg of next 2 rows, then dec 1 st at each end next row then every other row 5 times. (NOTE: while dec cable sts, k2tog across these 6 sts; actually dec 14 sts in all). Continue in pattern until work measures 25" (63.5cm) from beg. End with right side facing.

Shape Shoulders:
Bind off 14 sts at beg of next 4 rows (again k2tog across cable, losing 18 sts across each bind off row.) Bind off rem sts, k2tog across cable sts.

Front:
Work same as for back until armhole shaping is complete. End with right side facing.

Shape V-Neck:
Pattern across 68 (74) sts and turn. Working one side only, k 2 tog at beg of next row (neck edge) and work pattern to end. Dec 1 st at neck edge every other row until 36 sts rem. Work evenly in pattern until front measures same as back to shoulder shaping. End with right side facing.

Shape Shoulders:
Bind off 14 sts at beg of next row and then every other row once. (K 2 sts tog across cables. All 36 sts are now bound off.)

Join yarn to rem sts and work as for first side, reversing all shaping.

Neckband:
Sew right shoulder seam. With smaller needles and right side facing, pick up 68 sts down left front, 1 st from center (mark this st with a piece of yarn), 68 sts from right front and 42 sts across back neck. Work 6 rows in k1, p1 rib, k 3 center sts tog every row. Bind off loosely in rib.

Armbands:
Sew left shoulder seam. With smaller needles and right side facing, pick up 78 sts from each side of shoulder, 156 sts. Work 6 rows k1,p1 rib. *At the same time* k 2 tog at each end of every row. Bind off loosely in rib.

Finishing:
Sew side seams.

CLASSI-CALLY CABLE

This sweater has all the qualities of Cable News. It is extremely comfortable and warm, and equally suitable for men and women. Just remember to change the buttoning if you make it for a man.

Sizes:
This stitch gives the elastic quality of a rib. To fit 38 (40)″ / 96 (102)cm. Directions are for small/medium with medium/large in parentheses.

Materials:
17 50 gram balls of sportweight Shetland wool, or any sportweight yarn
6 buttons

Needles:
One pair each, size 2 (3mm), 3 (3.25mm) and 5 (4mm) knitting needles, or size needed to obtain gauge.

Gauge:
10 sts = 2″ (5cm) on #5 (4mm) needles over st st.

Abbreviations:
RT = Right Twist = k2tog, leave both sts on left hand needle, k 1st st again then sl both sts from needle tog.
C3 = Cable 3 = sl next 3 sts onto a cable needle and leave at front of work, k3, then k3 from cable needle.

Back:
With #3 (3.25mm) needles, cast on 97 (104) sts and work in pattern as follows:

Row 1: Sl 1, p1, * RT, p1, k1, p1, k1, p1. Rep from * to last 4 sts, then RT, p1, k1 tbl.
Row 2: Sl 1, k1, p2 * k1, p1, k1, p1, k1, p2. Rep from * to last 2 sts, k1, k1 tbl.

Rep these 2 rows until piece measures 1¾″ (4.5cm) from beg. End with the wrong side facing.

Next row: Sl 1, (k1, p1) into next st, p2 * (k1, p1) into the next 5 sts, p2. Rep from * to last 2 sts, then (k1, p1) into the next st, k1 tbl, 164 (176) sts.
Change to #5 (4mm) needles and work in pattern as follows:

Row 1: Sl 1, p2, * RT, p2, k6, p2. Rep from * to last 5 sts, RT, p2, k1 tbl.
Row 2: Sl 1, k2, p2, * k2, p6, k2, p2. Rep from * to last 3 sts, k2, k1 tbl.
Row 3: Sl 1, p2 * RT, p2, C3, p2. Rep from * to last 5 sts, RT, p2, k1 tbl.

Cont working row 1 for all right side rows and row 2 for all wrong side rows. Row 3 (cable) is repeated every 10th row. Work evenly in pattern until back measures 17″ (43cm) from beg. End with right side facing.

Shape Armhole:
Bind off 6 sts at the beg of the next 2 rows. (NOTE: When binding off in cable k2 sts tog across the 6 cable sts; actually dec 14 sts.) Dec 1 st at each end of the next row and then every other row 5 times, 126 (133) sts. Cont in pattern until piece measures 26″ (66cm) from the beg. End with right side facing.

Shape Shoulders:
Bind off 14 sts at the beg of the next 4 rows. (Again, when binding off cable sts k2tog, 18 sts in each bind off.) Then bind off rem 54 (61) sts. (Dec as before across cable sts.)

Pockets: (Make 2)
With #3 (3.25mm) needles, cast on 34 sts and work in st st for 5½″ (14cm). Place sts on holder.

Left Front:
With #3 (3.25mm) needles, cast on 56 (58) sts and work ribbing and front band as follows:

Row 1: Sl 1, p1 (3), * RT, p1, k1, p1, k1, p1. Rep from * to last 12 sts, RT, p1 (k1, p1) 4 times, k1 tbl.
Row 2: Sl 1, (k1, p1) 4 times, k1, p2, * k1, p1, k1, p1, k1, p2. Rep from * to last 2 (4) sts, k1 (3), k1 tbl.

Repeat these 2 rows until rib measures 1¾″ (4.5cm) from beg. Inc on last row as follows: Sl 1, rib 8, (k1, p1) in next st, p2, * (k1, p1) into next 5 sts, p2. Rep from * to last 2 (4) sts, (k1, p1) into next st (next 2 sts for larger size), k1 tbl, 88 (90) sts.

Change to #5 (4mm) needles and work in pattern as follows:

CLASSI-CALLY CABLE

Row 1: Sl 1, p2 (4) * RT, p2, k6, p2. Rep from * to last 13 sts, RT, p2 (k1, p1) 4 times, k1 tbl.
Row 2: Sl 1, rib 8, k2, p2, * K2, p6, k2, p2. Rep from * to last 3 (5) sts, k2 (4), k1 tbl.
Row 3: Sl 1, p2 (4), * RT, p2, C3, p2. Rep from * to last 13 sts, RT, p2 (k1, p1) 4 times, k1 tbl.

Cont working row 1 for all right side rows and row 2 for all wrong side rows. Row 3 (cable) is repeated every 10th row. Work evenly in pattern until piece measures 7" (18cm) from beg.

Insert pocket:
Sl 1, p2 (4), (RT, p2, k6 or C3 depending upon row, p2) twice, RT, sl next 34 sts onto a holder, pattern across sts from pocket, pattern and rib to end. Cont working in pattern until piece measures 16" (40.5cm) from beg. End with right side facing.

Front Shaping:
Pattern to last 11 sts, k2tog tbl, rib 8, k1 tbl. Work 1 row. Cont to dec every other row at front edge, *at the same time* when piece measures same as back to armhole, beg shaping.

Shape Armhole:
With right side facing, bind off 6 sts at beg of next row. (NOTE: Dec cables as for back.) Dec 1 st every other row 6 times, at armhole edge. Then work evenly at armhole edge, but cont to dec at neck edge, until piece measures same as for back to shoulder. End with right side facing.

Shape Shoulder:
Bind off 14 sts at beg of next row, then every other row once; knitting 2 sts tog across cables. Cont to rib on last 9 sts until band fits across to the center back. Bind off in rib.

Right Front:
Work as for left front, reversing all shaping. (NOTE: The front rib will now be at the beg of the row.) The insert pocket row will read: Sl 1, rib 8, pattern 16, sl 34 sts onto holder, pattern across 34 sts of 2nd pocket, pattern to end. Front Shaping: Sl 1, rib 8, k2tog. Make buttonholes in front rib to correspond to button placement. Make buttonholes: Sl 1, rib 3, yo, work 2 tog, rib 3, pattern to end.

Pocket Borders:
With #2 (3mm) needles, pick up 34 sts from pocket and work 4 rows in rib. Bind off in rib.

Sleeves (Make 2)
With #3 (3.25mm) needles, cast on 62 sts and work rib as for back, until piece measures 3½" (9cm) from beg. On last row inc as for back, 104 sts. Change to #5 (4mm) needles and pattern as for back. Inc 1 st at each end of 3rd row, then every 4th row until 152 sts, working inc sts into pattern. Work evenly until sleeve measures 18½" (47cm) from beg. End with right side facing.

Shape Cap:
Bind off 6 sts at beg of next 2 rows, always working 2 sts tog over cables. Dec 1 st at each end of every row until sleeve measures 23½" (60cm) from beg. End with wrong side facing. Bind off, k3 tog as you do.

Finishing:
Join shoulder seams and sew back neck section of front band into place. Set sleeves into armholes and sew into place. Sew pocket linings and pocket tops in place. Join side and sleeve seams.
Attach buttons to correspond to buttonholes.

CABLE BODIED

A new "slant" on cables. It's made in fingering weight yarn—and although I mention wool in the pattern, you can equally well use a mixed yarn, Shetland or lambs wool, as long as you follow the gauge. A wonderful wearable slipover vest—sure to give pleasure to all the men in your life.

Sizes:
To fit 38 (40, 42)" / 96 (102, 106)cm chest. Directions are for small with medium and large in parentheses.

Materials:
6 (6,7) 50 gram balls of fingering weight wool

Needles:
One pair each sizes 2 (3mm) and 3 (3.25mm) knitting needles or size needed to obtain gauge.

Gauge:
13 sts = 2" on size 3 (3.25mm) needles over st st.

Back:
With smaller needles, cast on 122 (130, 136) sts and work in k1, p1 rib for 3" (7.5cm). Inc 4 sts evenly across last row, 126 (134, 140) sts. Change to larger needles and work in st st until piece measures 16 (17, 17)" / 40.5 (43, 43)cm from cast on edge. End with right side facing.

Shape Armholes:
Bind off 8 (9, 10) sts at beg of next 2 rows. Then dec 1 st at each end of next row and then every other row until 90 (94, 98) sts rem. Continue in st st until piece measures 25½ (26½, 27½)" / 65 (67, 70)cm from cast on edge. End with right side facing.

Shape Shoulders:
Bind off 13 (14, 15) sts at beg of next 4 rows. Leave rem 38 sts on holder for neckband.

Front:
With smaller needles, cast on 122 (130, 136) sts and work in k1, p1 rib for 3" (7.5cm), inc 10 sts evenly across last row, 132 (140, 146) sts. Change to larger needles and work in pattern as follows:

Row 1: Sl 1, k1, p1, k8, p1, k39 (42, 44), p1, k8, p1, k39 (42, 44), p1, k8, p1, k21 (23, 25), k1 tbl.
Row 2: Sl 1, p21 (23, 25), k1, p8, k1, p39 (42, 44), k1, p8, k1, p39 (42, 44), k1, p8, k1, p1, k1 tbl.

Row 3: Sl 1, M1 (make 1 by knitting into front and back of next st), p1, k8, p1, k2tog, k36 (39, 41), M1, p1, k8, p1, k2tog, k36 (39, 41), M1, p1, k8, p1, k2tog, k19 (21, 23) k1 tbl.
Row 4: Sl 1, p20 (22, 24), k1, p8, k1, p39 (42, 44), k1, p8, k1, p39 (42, 44), k1, p8, k1, p2, k1 tbl.
Row 5: Sl 1, k1, M1, p1, k8, p1, k2tog, k36 (39, 41), M1, p1, k8, p1, k2tog, k36 (39,41), M1, p1, k8, p1, k2tog, k18 (20, 22), k1 tbl.
Row 6: Sl 1, p19 (21, 23), k1, p8, k1, p39 (42, 44), k1, p8, k1, p39 (42, 44), k1, p8, k1, p3, k1 tbl.
Row 7: Sl 1, k2, M1, p1, k8, p1, k2tog, k36 (39, 41), M1, p1, k8, p1, k2tog, k17 (19, 21), k1 tbl.
Row 8: Sl 1, p18 (20, 22), k1, p8, k1, p39 (42, 44), k1, p8, k1, p39 (42, 44), k1, p8, k1, p4, k1 tbl.
Row 9: Sl 1, k3, M1, p1, k8, p1, k2tog, k36 (39, 41), M1, p1, k8, p1, k2tog, k16 (18, 20), k1 tbl.
Row 10: Sl 1, p17 (19, 21), k1, p8, k1, p39 (42, 44), k1, p8, k1, p39 (42, 44), k1, p8, k1, p5, k1 tbl.
Row 11: Sl 1, k4, M1, p1, C8 (sl next 4 sts onto cable needle and leave in back of work, k4, then k4 from cable needle.), p1, k2tog, k36 (39, 41), M1, p1, C8, p1, k2tog, k36 (39, 41), M1, p1, C8, p1, k2tog, k15 (17, 19), k1 tbl.
Row 12: Sl 1, p16 (18, 20), k1, p8, k1, p39 (42, 44), k1, p8, k1, p39 (42, 44), k1, p8, k1, p6, k1 tbl.

Cable sts move across on every alternate row by M1 before cable sts and k2tog after. Cont in this way working C8 on every 10th row. When 42 (45, 47) sts in st st begin the row, start cable pattern as follows:

Row 1: Sl 1, k1, p1, k39 (42, 44) pattern to end.
Row 2: Pattern to last 42 (45, 47) sts, p39 (42, 44), k1, p1, k1 tbl.
Row 3: Sl 1, M1, p1, k2tog, k37 (40, 42), pattern to end.

CABLE BODIED

Row 4: Pattern to last 42 (45, 47) sts, p38 (41, 43), k1, p2, k1 tbl.

Row 5: Sl 1, M1, k1, p1, k2tog, k36 (39, 41), pattern to end.

Row 6: Pattern to last 42 (45, 47) sts, p37 (40, 42), k1, p2, k1, k1 tbl.

Row 7: Sl 1, M1, p2, k1, k2tog, k35 (38, 40) pattern to end.

Row 8: Pattern to last 42 (45, 47), p36 (39, 41), k1, p3, k1, k1 tbl.

Cont in this pattern until complete cable (10 sts) is set, then work in pattern as before until piece measures 16 (17, 17)" / 40.5 (43, 43)cm from cast on edge. End with right side facing.

Shape Armholes:

Cont to work in cable slope pattern and bind off 8 (9, 10) sts at beg of next 2 rows.

Shape "V" Neck:

Pattern 58 (61, 63) sts and turn. Working on this side only, work one row. Then dec 1 st at armhole edge on next and then every other row 10 (11, 11) times—*at the same time*—dec 1 st at neck edge on next and then every 3rd row until 30 (34, 38) sts rem. (NOTE: When 29 (31, 32) sts in st st beg row, start another cable as before.) Then dec every other row at neck edge until 22 (24, 26) sts rem. Cont in pattern until work measures 25½ (26½, 27½)" / 65 (67, 70)cm from cast on edge. End with right side facing.

Shape Shoulders:

Cont working in pattern and bind off 11 (12, 13) sts at beg of next and following alt row. Join yarn to rem sts and work to match first side, reversing all shaping and continuing in slope cable pattern.

Neckband:

Sew right shoulder seam. With smaller needles and right side facing, pick up and k75 sts down left side of front neck, 1 st from center front, 75 sts up right side of front neck and 38 sts from back—189 sts. Work 6 rows in k1, p1 rib; dec 1 st each side of center front st on every row. Bind off in rib.

Armbands:

Sew left shoulder and neckband seam. With smaller needles and right side facing, pick up and k188 sts evenly around armhole edge. (Have sts slightly further apart on 1" of each side of shoulder seam to prevent puckering.) Work 6 rows in k1, p1 rib. Bind off in rib.

Finishing:

Sew side seams.

18

NATURAL CHARM

This snugly fitting lightweight cardigan with floral stitch trim is a delightful companion to full skirts or dresses. Again, any fingering weight yarn can be used. Its simplicity is its charm.

Sizes:

To fit 32 (34, 36)" / 81 (86, 91)cm bust. Directions are for small with medium and large in parentheses.

Materials:

7 50 gram balls of fingering weight yarn
10 buttons

Needles:

One pair each sizes 2 (3mm) and 3 (3.25mm) knitting needles or size needed to obtain gauge.

Gauge:

14 sts = 2" over st st on #3 (3.25mm) needles.

Abbreviations:

TW2F = Twist 2 front = Take the needle in front of first st on left hand needle and k the 2nd st. Now p into back of 1st st, sl both sts off needle tog.
TW2B = Twist 2 back = Take the needle behind the first st on left hand needle and p into back of second st. Now k into front of 1st st. Sl both sts off needle tog.

Back:

With smaller needles cast on 98 (106, 110) sts and work in k2, p2 rib for 3½" (9cm). Next row: P9 (7, 6) sts * inc in next st, p13 (15, 12) rep from * to last 11 (9, 8) sts. Following row: P across 105 (113, 119) sts. Change to larger needles and pattern as follows:

Row 1: (wrong side facing) Knit.
Row 2: (right side facing) Purl.
Row 3: Knit
Row 4: Sl 1, * yo, k2tog, rep from * to end.
Row 5: Knit
Row 6: Purl
Row 7: Knit
Row 8: Sl 1, p8 (12, 15), k3, * p9, k3, rep from * to last 9 (13, 16) sts, p8 (12, 15), k1 tbl.
Row 9: Sl 1, k8 (12, 15), p3, * k9, p3. Rep from * to last 9 (13, 16) sts, k8 (12, 15), k1 tbl.
Row 10: Repeat row 8.
Row 11: Repeat row 9.
Row 12: Sl 1, p7 (11, 14), * TW2F, k1, TW2B, p7. Rep from * to last 1 (5, 8) sts, p0 (4, 7), k1 tbl.

Row 13: Sl 1, k7 (11, 14), * (p1, k1) twice, p1, k7. Rep from * to last 1 (5, 8) sts. k0 (4, 7), k1 tbl.
Row 14: Sl 1, p6 (10, 13), * TW2F, p1, k1, p1, TW2B, p5. Rep from * to last 2 (6, 9) sts, p1 (5, 8), k1 tbl.
Row 15: Sl 1, k6, (10, 13), * (p1, k2) twice, p1, k5. Rep from * to last 2 (6, 9) sts, k1 (5, 8), k1 tbl.
Row 16: Sl 1, p5 (9, 12), * TW2F, p2, k1, p2, TW2B, p3. Rep from * to last 3 (7, 10) sts, p2 (6, 9), k1 tbl.
Row 17: Sl 1, k5 (9, 12), * p1, k3. Rep from * to last 3 (7, 10) sts. K2 (6, 9), k1 tbl.
Row 18: Sl 1, p5 (9, 12), * (k1, p1, k1, p1, k1) into next st (making 5 sts in one), p3, k1, p3, (k1, p1, k1, p1, k1) into next st, p3. Rep from * to last 3 (7, 10) sts. P2 (6, 9), k1 tbl.
Row 19: Sl 1, k5 (9, 12), * p5, k3, p1, k3, p5, k3. Rep from * to last 3 (7, 10) sts. K2 (6, 9), k1 tbl.
Row 20: Sl 1, p5 (9, 12), * k5, p3 (k1, p1, k1, p1, k1) into next st, p3, k5, p3. Rep from * to last 3 (7, 10) sts. P2 (6, 9), k1 tbl.
Row 21: Sl 1, k5 (9, 12), * p5, k3. Rep from * to last 3 (7, 10) sts. K2 (6, 9), k1 tbl.
Row 22: Sl 1, p5 (9, 12), * k5tog, p3, k5, p3, k5tog, p3. Rep from * to last 3 (7, 10) sts. P2 (6, 9), k1 tbl.
Row 23: Sl 1, k5 (9, 12), * k4, p5, k7. Rep from * to last 3 (7, 10) sts. K2 (6, 9), k1 tbl.
Row 24: Sl 1, p5 (9, 12), * k1, p3, k5tog, p3, k1, p3. Rep from * to last 3 (7, 10) sts. P2 (6, 9), k1 tbl.

Cont in st st. Inc 1 st at each end of every 12th row until 113 (121, 127) sts. Work evenly until piece measures 13½" (34cm).

NATURAL CHARM

Shape Armhole:

Bind off 6 (8, 8) sts at beg of next 2 rows. Dec 1 st at each end of next 5 (5, 7) rows, then every other row 5 (5, 5) times, 81 (85, 87) sts. Work evenly until piece measures 19½" (49.5cm).

Shape Neck:

Work across 29 (31, 32) sts, bind off 23 sts loosely and work to end of row. Working one side only, dec 1 st at neck edge on next 2 (2, 4) rows then every other row once. Work evenly until piece measures 21" (53cm).

Shape Shoulder:

Beg with shoulder edge, bind off 6, (7, 7) sts at beg of row. Dec 1 st at neck edge on next row. Bind off 8 (9, 9) sts at beg of next row. Work one row. Bind off rem sts. Join yarn to rem sts at neck edge. Work these sts to correspond to first side, reversing all shaping. (NOTE: work one row more before shoulder shaping.)

First Front:

With smaller needles cast on 46 (48, 48) sts and work in k2, p2 rib for 3½" (9cm). Next row: p. Foll row: p across inc 4 (4, 6) sts evenly across row, 50 (52, 54) sts. Change to larger needles and work in pattern as follows:

Row 1: (wrong side) Knit.
Row 2: (right side) Purl.
Row 3: Knit.
Row 4: Sl 1, * yo, k2tog. Rep from * to end.
Row 5: Knit.
Row 6: Purl.
Row 7: Knit.
Row 8: Sl 1, p4 (5, 6), k3, * p9, k3. Rep from * to last 6, (7, 8) sts, p5 (6, 7), k1 tbl.
Row 9: Sl 1, k5 (6, 7), p3, * k9, p3. Rep from * to last 5 (6, 7) sts, k4 (5, 6), k1 tbl.
Row 10: Repeat row 8.
Row 11: Repeat row 9.

Row 12: Sl 1, p3 (4, 5), * TW2F, k1, TW2B, p7. Rep from * to last 10 (11, 12) sts, TW2F, k1, TW2B, p4 (5, 6), k1 tbl.
Row 13: Sl 1, k4 (5, 6), * (p1, k1) twice, p1, k7. Rep from * to last 9 (10, 11) sts, p1, k1, p1, k1, k3 (4, 5), k1 tbl.
Row 14: Sl 1, p2 (3, 4), * TW2F, p1, k1, p1, TW2B, p5. Rep from * to last 11 (12, 13) sts, TW2F, p1, k1, p1, TW2B, p3 (4, 5), k1 tbl.
Row 15: Sl 1, k3 (4, 5), * (p1, k2) twice, p1, k5. Rep from * to last 10 (11, 12) sts, p1, k2, p1, k2, p1, k2 (3, 4), k1 tbl.
Row 16: Sl 1, p1 (2, 3), * TW2F, p2, k1, p2, TW2B, p3. Rep from * to last 12 (13, 14) sts, TW2F, p2, k1, p2, TW2B, p2 (3, 4), k1 tbl.
Row 17: Sl 1, k2 (3, 4), * p1, k3. Rep from * to last 11 (12, 13) sts, p1, (k3) twice, p1, k1 (2, 3), k1, tbl.
Row 18: Sl 1, p1 (2, 3), * (k1, p1, k1, p1, k1) into next st, p3, k1, p3, (k1, p1, k1, p1, k1) into next st, p3. Rep from * to last 12 (13, 14) sts, (k1, p1, k1, p1, k1) into the next st, p3, k1, p3 (k1, p1, k1, p1, k1) into the next st, p2 (3, 4), k1 tbl.
Row 19: Sl 1, k2 (3, 4), * p5, k3, p1, k3, p5, k3. Rep from * to last 19 (20, 21) sts, p5, k3, p1, k3, p5, k1 (2, 3), k1 tbl.
Row 20: Sl 1, p1 (2, 3), * k5, p3, (k1, p1, k1, p1, k1) into next st, p3, k5, p3. Rep from * to last 20 (21, 22) sts, k5, p3, (k1, p1, k1, p1, k1) into next st, p3, k5, p2 (3, 4), k1 tbl.
Row 21: Sl 1, k2 (3, 4), * p5, k3. Rep from * to last 7 (8, 9) sts, p5, k1 (2, 3), k1 tbl.
Row 22: Sl 1, p1 (2, 3), * k5tog, p3, k5, p3, k5tog, p3. Rep from * to last 24 (25, 26) sts, k5tog, p3, k5, p3, k5tog, p2 (3, 4), k1 tbl.
Row 23: Sl 1, k2 (3, 4), * k4, p5, k7. Rep from * to last 15 (16, 17) sts, k4, p5, k5 (6, 7), k1 tbl.
Row 24: Sl 1, p1 (2, 3), * k1, p3, k5 tog, p3, k1, p3. Rep from * to last 16 (17, 18) sts, k1, p3, k5tog, p3, k1, p2 (3, 4), k1 tbl.

Now cont in st st, inc 1 st at side edge on every 12th row until there are 54 (56, 59) sts. Work until front measures same as back to armhole shaping.

Shape Armhole:

Beg at side edge and bind off 6 (8, 8) sts at beg of next row. Dec 1 st at armhole edge every row 5 (5, 7) times; then every other row 5 (5, 5) times, 38 (38, 39) sts. Work evenly until piece measures 18" (46cm).

Shape Neck:

Beg with neck edge and bind off 4 (3, 4) sts at beg of row, then dec 1 st at neck edge every other row until 25 (27, 27) sts remain. Work in st st until same length as back to shoulder shaping.

Shape Shoulder:

Beg with side edge and bind off 7 (7, 7) sts at beg of row. Work 1 row. Bind off 8 (9, 9) sts at beg of next row. Work 1 row. Bind off rem 10 (11, 11) sts.

Second Front:

Work as for first front, reversing all shaping.

Sleeves:

With smaller needles cast on 50 (54, 54) sts and work in k2, p2 rib for 4″ (10cm). Inc 31 sts evenly spaced across next row, 81 (85, 85) sts. Change to larger needles and pattern row 1 thru 7, as for back.
Row 8: Sl 1, p8 (10, 10), k3, * p9, k3. Rep from * to last 9 (11, 11) sts, p8 (10, 10), k1 tbl.

Cont in pattern as established and work one complete pattern (24 rows). Change to st st and inc 1 st at each end of next and then every 12th row until there are 87 (91, 91) sts. Work evenly until sleeve measures 17½″ (44.5cm).

Shape Cap:

Bind off 6 (8, 8) sts at beg of next 2 rows. Dec 1 st at each end of next row and then every other row until 23 sts rem. Bind off.

Front Band:

With smaller needles, cast on 12 sts and work in rib as follows:

Row 1: Sl 1, k1, p2, k2, p2, k2, p1, k1 tbl.
Row 2: Sl 1, k1, p1, k2, p2, k2, p1, k1 tbl.

Work rows 1 and 2 until band fits up left front of cardigan, slightly stretched. (approx 17–17½″/43–44.5cm) Leave sts on holder.

Buttonhole band:

Work as for button band, making a buttonhole on 5th row.
Buttonhole: Rib 5, bind off 2 sts, rib to end. Rib 5, cast on 2 sts, rib to end.
Work 8 more buttonholes 2″ apart (the last buttonhole should be placed ½″ below the end of band.) Place sts on holder.

Neckband:

Sew shoulder seams. With right side facing, pick up rib sts from right band, 26 sts up front, 62 sts across back, 26 sts down front, and sts from button band. Work 5 rows in garter st. Work a buttonhole as before on next row. Work 2 rows in garter st. Bind off loosely.

Finishing:

Sew front bands in place. Pin sleeves in place, matching pattern with fullness at shoulder edge. Sew in place. Sew side and sleeve seams. Sew on buttons.

DISCREET CHARM

One of my top favorites, this combines three of the best known stitches—seed, cable and diamond. It looks particularly beautiful if you use the soft heathery tones of Shetland wool.

Sizes:
To fit 32(34, 36)″ / 81(86, 91) cm bust. Directions are for small with larger sizes in parentheses.

Materials:
7(7, 8) 50 gm balls of fingering weight Shetland wool or any fingering weight yarn
3 buttons

Needles:
One pair each size 1 (2.50mm) and size 3 (3.25mm) knitting needles, or size needed to obtain gauge.

Gauge:
15 sts = 2″ (5cm) on #3 needles worked over 12 rows of pattern.

Back:
With smaller needles, cast on 118(122, 130) sts and work in k2, p2 rib for 3½″ (9cm). Inc 7 sts evenly spaced across last row of rib, 125(129, 137) sts. Change to larger needles and pattern as follows:

Row 1: (p1, k1) 3(4, 6) times, p1 * k6, (p1, k1) 7 times p1, repeat from * 4 times more, k6 (p1, k1) 3(4, 6) times p1.
Row 2: (p1, k1) 3(4, 6) times p1, * p6 (p1, k1) 3 times p3 (k1, p1) 3 times, repeat from * 4 times more, p6 (p1, k1) 3(4, 6) times p1.
Row 3: (p1, k1) 3(4, 6) times p1 * k6 (p1, k1) twice, p1, k5, p1 (k1, p1) twice, repeat from * 4 times more, k6, (p1, k1) 3(4, 6) times p1.
Row 4: (p1, k1) 3(4, 6) times, p1 * p6 (p1, k1) twice, p7 (k1, p1) twice, repeat from * 4 times more, p6, (p1, k1) 3(4, 6) times p1
Row 5: (p1, k1) 3(4, 6) times p1 * slip next 3 sts onto a cable needle and leave at back of work, knit next 3 sts, then knit 3 sts from the cable needle, p1, k1, p1, k9, p1, k1, p1 repeat from * 4 times more, cable next 6 sts as before (p1, k1) 3(4, 6) times p1
Row 6: (p1, k1) 3(4, 6) times p1 * p6, p1, k1, p11, k1, p1, repeat from * 4 times more, p6 (p1, k1) 3(4, 6) times p1
Row 7: (p1, k1) 3(4, 6) times p1 * k6, p1, k1, p1, k9, p1, k1, p1, repeat from * 4 times more, k6, (p1, k1) 3(4, 6) times p1

Row 8: As 4th.
Row 9: As 3rd.
Row 10: As 2nd.
Row 11: (p1, k1) 3(4, 6) times p1 * Cable 6, (p1, k1) 7 times, p1, repeat from * 4 times more, Cable 6, (p1, k1) 3(4, 6) times p1
Row 12: (p1, k1) 3(4, 6) times p1 * p6 (p1, k1) 7 times, p1, repeat from * 4 times more, p6, (p1, k1) 3(4, 6) times p1.

These 12 rows form pattern. Cont in pattern until work measures 14(14½, 15½)″ / 36(37, 39)cm from beg. End with right side facing.

Shape Armholes:
Keep pattern correct and bind off 6 sts at beg of next 2 rows, then dec 1 st each side of every row until 107(109, 113) sts rem. Work evenly until piece measures 21½(21½, 22)″ / 54.5(54.5, 56)cm from beg. End with right side facing.

Shape Shoulders:
Bind off 17(17, 18) sts at beg of next 4 rows. Place rem sts onto holder for neckband.

Front:
Work as for back until front measures 19½(20, 20½)″ / 49.5(51, 52)cm from beg. End with right side facing.

Shape Neck:
Keep pattern correct and work across 38(39, 41) sts, turn, and cont on these sts and dec 1 st at neck edge every row until 34(34, 36) sts rem. Work evenly until piece measures same as back to shoulder. End with right side facing.

DISCREET CHARM

Shape Shoulder:
Bind off 17(17, 18) sts at beg of next row and then every other row once. S1 31 center sts onto holder for neckband. Join yarn to rem sts and work to match first side.

Sleeves:
With smaller needles, cast on 56 sts and work in k2, p2 rib for 3½" (9cm). Inc 15 sts evenly spaced across last row, 71 sts. Change to larger needles and set pattern as follows:
Row 1: S1 1 * k6,(p1, k1) 7 times, p1, rep from * twice more k6, k1, tbl. (Working center pattern only to begin with.) *At the same time*, inc 1 st each end of 5th and every following 6th row until there are 83 sts, work all increased sts in seed st. Work evenly until sleeve measures 18½" (47cm) from beg.

Shape Cap
Bind off 4 sts at beg of next 2 rows, then dec 1 st at each end of every other row until 33 sts rem. Then dec 1 st at each end every row until 23 sts rem. Working 2 sts tog, bind off.

Neckband:
Sew right shoulder seam. With right side facing, smaller needles start at left shoulder, pick up 24 sts down left front, 31 sts from center front, 24 sts up right front, and sts from center back. Work in k2, p2 rib for 6 rows. Bind off in rib.

Finishing:
Sew left shoulder seam, leaving 3" (7.5cm) open at neck edge. Attach buttons to back of this opening and crochet chain st loops on front to fit buttons. Set sleeves into armhole and sew into place. Join side and sleeve seams.

NOTE: Avoid blocking this sweater, as the texture will flatten.

Country Casuals

This section includes sweaters inspired by very old samplers which are stylish additions to any fashion look. They can be dressed up with antique lace and velvets—or worn with your favorite jeans and soft skirts. Whatever look you favor, they will always be *the* special accessory in your wardrobe. ▪ For these samplers I have specified the colors used for the originals, but only as a guide. There is no reason that you should not use any colors you have at hand. It does not even matter what type of yarn you use— mohair, or even a touch of lurex here and there. It's great fun and a wonderful opportunity to use up your bits and pieces. ▪ When working with several different colors for motifs, it is easier to use manageable lengths of each color rather than whole balls as this prevents tangling. *Always* twist yarns round each other at every color change to prevent holes. With larger motifs it is best not to carry or "float" the base yarn across; either keep a ball or length on either side, or break it off each time. To make these garments look really professional, the motifs should lie absolutely flat with no pulling or puckering. ▪ These are superb sweaters for all seasons and some of them are real collector's pieces.

COUNTRY LIFE

A delightful little cardigan, this will excite comment whenever you wear it. It is one of my very special favorites.

Sizes:
Finished measurements 32 (34, 36, 38)" / 81 (86, 91, 96)cm. Directions are for petite with small, medium and large in parentheses.

Materials:
9 (9, 10) 50 gm balls fingering weight Shetland wool in MC
Small amounts in 12 CC (pale green, gold, light pink, red, brown, wine, pilot blue, bright pink, bottle green, black, cream and moss green)
9 buttons

Needles:
One pair each size 1 (2.50mm) and size 4 (3.50mm), or size needed to obtain gauge.

Gauge:
14 sts and 16 rows = 2" (5cm) square on #4 (3.50mm) needles over st st.

Back:
With smaller needles and MC, cast on 100 (104, 108, 112) sts and work in k1, p1 rib for 2½" (6cm). Inc 14 (16, 18, 20) sts evenly spaced across last row, 114 (120, 126, 132) sts. Change to larger needles and work in st st until piece measures 13½" (34cm) from beg.

Shape Armholes:
Bind off 4 sts at beg of the next 2 rows. Then dec 1 st at each end of every other row until there are 98 (102, 106, 110) sts. Work evenly until piece measures 22½ (23, 23½, 24)" / 57 (58.5, 60, 61cm) from beg. End with right side facing.

Shape Shoulders:
Bind off 15 (16, 17, 18) sts at beg of next 4 rows. Place rem 38 sts on a holder for neckband.

Left Front:
With smaller needles and MC, cast on 57 (59, 61, 63) sts and work in k1, p1 rib for 2½" (6cm). On the last row place 7 sts at front edge on holder, and inc 8 sts evenly spaced across row, 58 (60, 62, 64) sts. Change to larger needles and work in st st until piece measures 7" (18cm) from beg. End with right side facing. Set chart A as follows: work 0 (2, 4, 6) sts, then work across 51 sts of chart, knit to end. With pattern set, work 28 rows of chart. Cont in MC until piece measures 12" (30.5cm). End with right side facing. Work Fair Isle band B. When band is complete work in MC until piece measures same as back to armhole shaping. End at armhole edge.

Shape Armhole:
Bind off 4 sts at beg of next and then every other row once, 50 (52, 54, 56) sts. Work across 47 sts of chart C, then work 3 (5, 7, 9) sts. When chart C is complete work Fair Isle band D. Then work in MC until piece measures 5½" (14cm) from start of armhole shaping. End at side edge. Follow 18 sts of chart E across row.

Neck Shaping:
At the same time place 13 sts from center front on holder. Dec 1 st neck edge every other row 7 times.

Shape Shoulder:
Bind off 15 (16, 17, 18) sts at beg of next row and then every other row once.

Right Front:
Work as for left front, reversing all shaping, until 5th row, make buttonhole as follows: Sl 1, rib 2, yo, work 2 sts tog, rib to end. Cont to work as for left front until piece measures 7" (18cm) from beg. Work chart F, working the extra sts in MC at side edge. When chart is complete work in MC until piece measures same as left front to Fair Isle pattern. Work Fair Isle chart B, then work in MC until piece measures same as left front to armhole shaping.

COUNTRY LIFE

Shape Armhole:

Bind off 4 sts at beg of next row and then every other row once. Work chart G, followed by Fair Isle band D to match left front. Complete right front as for left front, reversing all shaping and placing of 18 sts of chart E across row.

Left Sleeve:

With smaller needles and MC, cast on 46 (48, 50, 52) sts and work k1, p1 rib for 2½" (6cm). Inc 26 (28, 30, 32) sts evenly spaced across last row, 72 (76, 80, 84) sts. Change to larger needles and follow 2 rows of chart L. Work 2 rows in MC, then work 18 sts rep of chart E (hearts), leaving 0 (2, 4, 6) sts of MC on either side. When chart E is complete work 2 rows in MC, then 7 center rows of Fair Isle band D. Work 1" (2.5cm) in MC. Work in chart J as follows: Sl 1, k35 (37, 39, 41) sts in MC, work across 22 sts of chart, k in MC to end. When pattern is complete work in MC, inc 1 st at each end of next row and then every 4th row until there are 96 (96, 104, 104) sts. Work evenly until sleeve measures 18" (46cm) from beg.

Shape Cap:

Bind off 4 sts at the beg of the next 2 rows. Dec 1 st at each end of every other row until 68 (68, 64, 64) sts rem. Then dec 1 st each side every row until 36 sts rem. Bind off knitting 3 sts tog across row.

Right Sleeve:

Work as for left sleeve, omitting chart J (donkey). When sleeve measures 16" (40.5cm), end with right side facing and set chart K as follows: k40 (42, 44, 46) sts, work across 7 sts of pattern (chicken feet), k in MC to end. With pattern set, finish as for first sleeve.

Left Front Band:

With smaller needles, pick up 7 sts left on holder and cont in rib, until band fits up the front, slightly stretched. With pins, mark the positions of the 9 buttons (the last one should come in the neckband).

Right Front Band:

Work as for left band, but make buttonholes (as before) to correspond to button positions. Sew shoulder seams.

Neckband:

With right side facing, smaller needles and MC pick up 7 sts from right front band, 13 sts from right center front, 18 (19, 20, 21) sts up right side, 38 sts from back, 18 (19, 20, 21) sts down left side, 13 sts from left center and 7 sts from left front band. Work in k1, p1 rib for 3 rows. Make a buttonhole at the beg of the next row, rib two more rows. Bind off in rib.

Finishing

Sew in all ends. Sew front bands into place. Set sleeves into armholes, easing any fullness at top, evenly, at each side of the shoulder seam. Attach buttons to left front band to correspond with buttonholes.

COUNTRY LIFE

Base = Navy
X = Red
● = Light Brown
/ = Moss Green
I = Pilot Blue
○ = Wine
• = White
∨ = Pale Green
◇ = Gold
▼ = Bottle Green
\ = Bright Pink
◢ = Flesh Pink

ALTERNATELY USE A VERY
PALE GREEN AS BASE COLOR
THEN CHANGING Z = WHITE,
OTHER COLORS THE SAME.

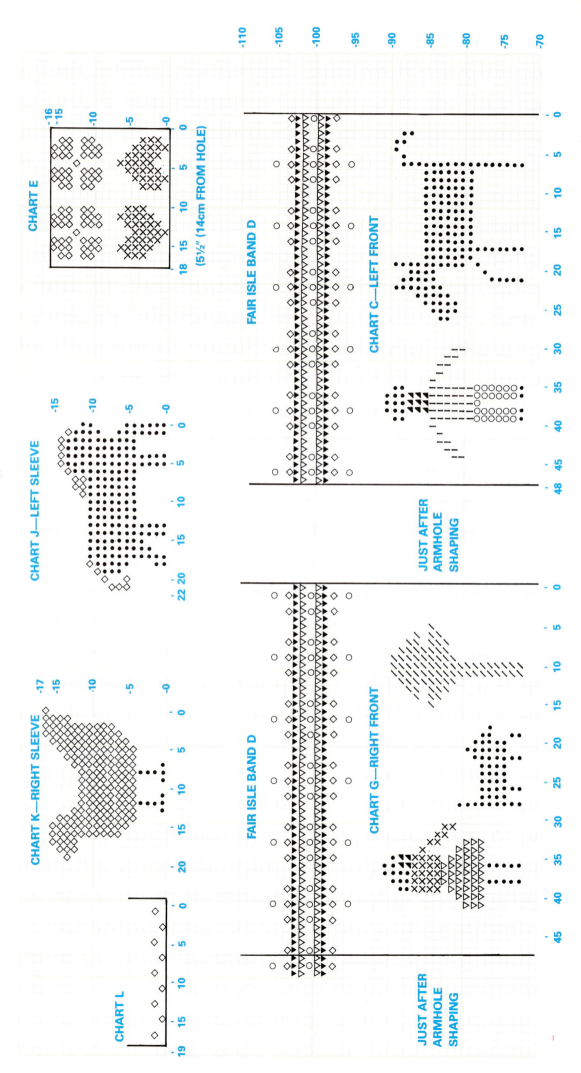

CHART E

(5½" (14cm FROM HOLE)

FAIR ISLE BAND D

CHART C—LEFT FRONT

JUST AFTER ARMHOLE SHAPING

CHART J—LEFT SLEEVE

CHART K—RIGHT SLEEVE

CHART L

FAIR ISLE BAND D

CHART G—RIGHT FRONT

JUST AFTER ARMHOLE SHAPING

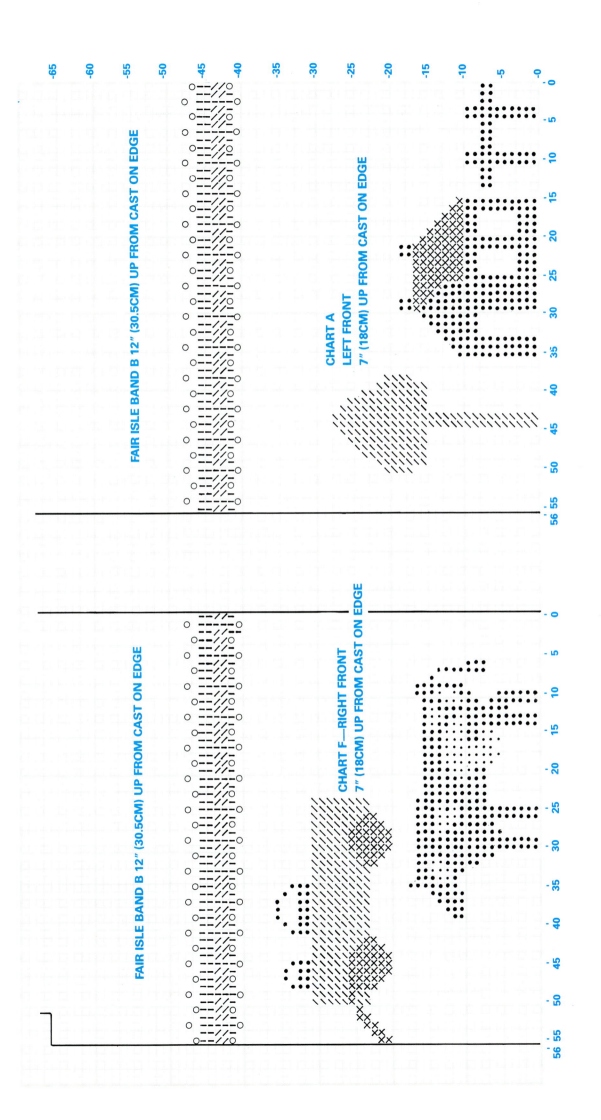

FAIR ISLE BAND B 12" (30.5CM) UP FROM CAST ON EDGE

CHART A
LEFT FRONT
7" (18CM) UP FROM CAST ON EDGE

FAIR ISLE BAND B 12" (30.5CM) UP FROM CAST ON EDGE

CHART F—RIGHT FRONT
7" (18CM) UP FROM CAST ON EDGE

FLORAL REFLECTIONS

This mixture of old lace and tapestry is not the easiest of garments to knit, but it's well worth the effort. To keep the really antique look use colors of the same soft tones.

Sizes:
To fit 32 (34,36)" /81 (86,91)cm bust. Directions are for small with medium and large in parentheses. Finished bust measurements 35 (37,39)" /89 (94,99)cm.

Materials:
Light weight Shetland wool
6 50 gm balls of beige MC
3 50 gm balls of pale pink CC (for lace pattern)
1 ball each of moss green, mauve, rose pink, grass green, soft rust, dark pink, soft blue, gold, cream
3 buttons

Needles:
One pair each size 1 (2.50mm) and size 3 (3.25mm) or size needed to obtain gauge.

Gauge:
18 sts = 2½" (6cms) on #3 needles worked in st st over lace pattern.

Back:
With size 1 (2.50mm) needles, cast on 100 (108, 116) sts. Work k1, p1, rib for 3" (7.5cms). Inc 26 sts evenly spaced across the last row, 126 (134, 142) sts. Change to #3 (3.25) needles and work in st st (k1 row p1 row) for 2 rows. *Next row* begin lace pattern by following chart. Repeat these 16 rows 5 times. (Five complete patterns to armhole.)

Shape Armholes:
Continue working in lace pattern, *at the same time* bind off 4 sts at the beg of the next 2 rows. Then dec 1 st each end every other row 8 (9,10) times, until 102 (108,114) sts remain. Work even in pattern until armhole measures 7½ (8,8½)"/19 (20,21.5cms).

Shape Shoulders:
Bind off 16 (17,18) sts at the beg of the next 4 rows. Place the rem 38 (40,42) sts on a holder for the neckband.

Front:
Work the same as for back until row 19—then following chart, begin floral pattern. Follow chart working the armholes same as for back, until floral pattern is completed. Work next three rows according to chart. Then, bind off center 30 (32, 34) sts. Attach yarn and work both

sides of the neck at once. Continuing in lace pattern, dec 1 st each side of neck edge every other row 4 times. Work even on rem 32 (34, 36) sts (each side), until front measures same as back. Bind off 32 (34, 36) sts from armhole edge.

Sleeves:
With size 1 (2.50mm) needles, cast on 54 (56, 58) sts and work in k1, p1 rib for 3" (7.5cms). Inc 18 sts evenly spaced across last row. Change to #3 needles and work pattern as for back. *At the same time*: Inc 1 st at each end on the 13th row. Then every 6th row inc 1 st each end, until 108 (112, 116) sts. Work even until sleeve measures 18" (46cms) or until desired length of sleeve to underarm.

Shape Cap:
Bind off 6 sts at the beg of the next 4 rows, 84 (88, 92) sts. Then dec 1 st at each end every other row until 48 (50, 52) sts remain. P 1 row. *Next row*: With MC only k3tog all along row. Next row bind off.

Neckband:
Join right shoulder seam. With MC and size 1 needles hold sweater with right side facing and pick up 18 (20, 22) sts down left front, 30 (32, 34) sts from neck, 18 (20, 22) sts up right front, and 38 (40, 42) sts across back. Work 6 rows in k1, p1 rib. Bind off loosely in rib.

Finishing:
Join left shoulder seam leaving the neck open for 2½" (6cms). Sew 3 buttons to the back of this opening. Crochet chain st loops to fit buttons. Set in sleeves and sew into place. Weave in ends. Join side and sleeve seams. If desired sweater may be blocked.

FLORAL REFLECTIONS

Base = Pale Pink
- × = Stone
- ● = Moss Green
- ○ = Dk Pink
- ▼ = Soft Blue
- ◇ = Cream
- ▽ = Soft Rust
- \ = Mauve
- / = Gold
- — = Grass Green
- ◣ = Rose Pink

A VERY SOFT GREEN BASE
WAS ALSO USED WITH SAME
CONTRAST COLORS.

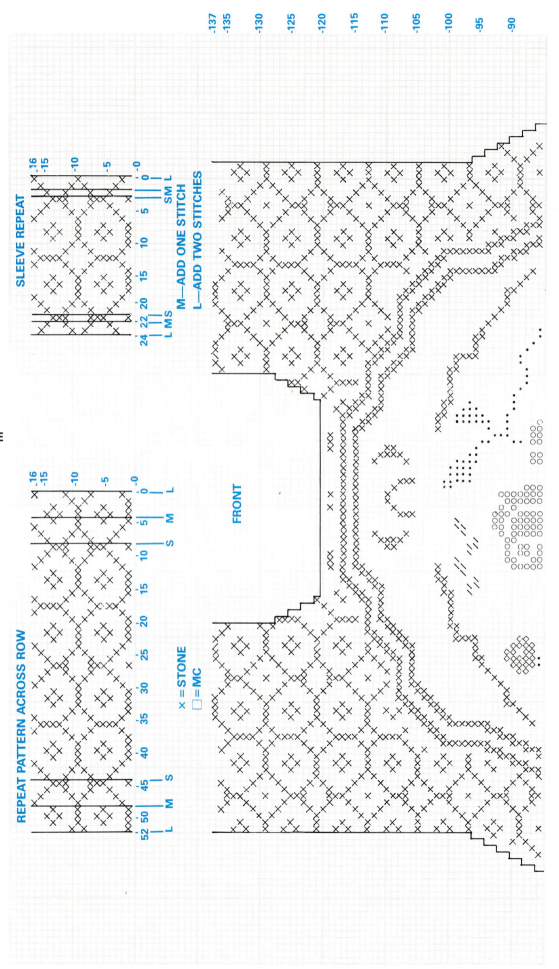

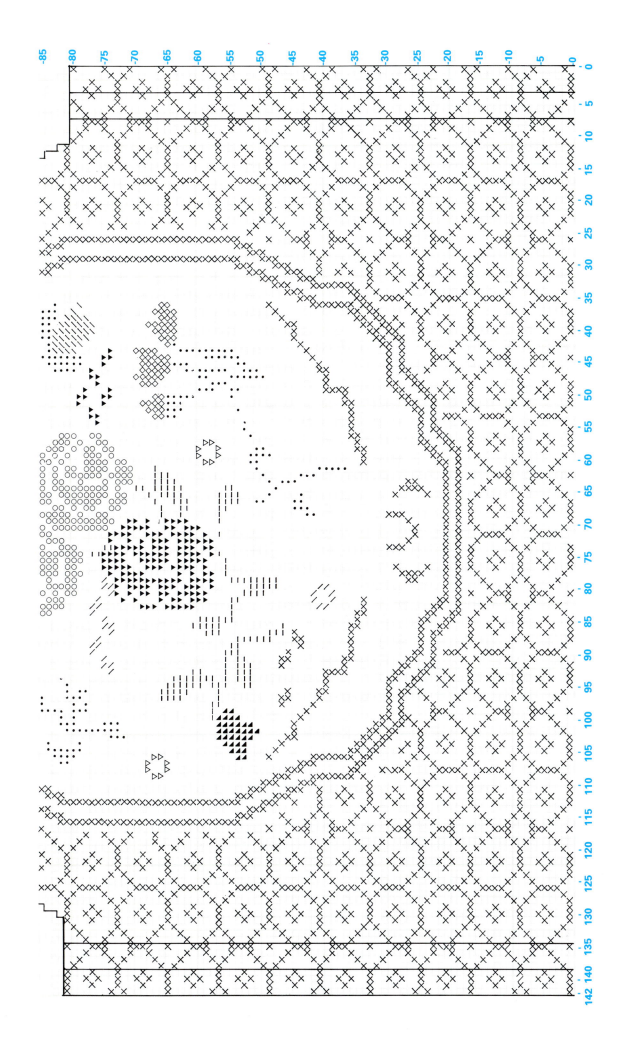

EASY ELEGANCE

A casual but elegant long cardigan. For this I have knitted 2 strands of fingering weight yarn together. You can use 2 strands of pure wool, or 1 strand of wool and 1 of cotton. If you use the mixture, you'll find that the wool helps to keep the cotton in shape. Soft subtle shades are best; they give the piece a fashionable and tweedy look.
The cable adds some eye-catching interest.

Sizes:
To be worn loose. Finished bust measurements approximately 40 (44, 46)" / 102 (112, 117)cm. Directions are for small with medium and large in parentheses.

Materials:
9 (9,10) 50 gm balls of fingering weight wool in 2 colors
2 buttons

Needles:
One pair each size 5 (3.75 mm) and size 7 (4.50 mm) knitting needles, or size needed to obtain gauge.

Gauge:
25 sts = 4" (10cm) over st st on #7 needles

Abbreviations:
C16 = Cable 16 = Sl next 4 sts onto cable needle and leave at back of work, k4, k4 from cable needle, sl next 4 sts onto cable needle and hold in front of work, k4, k4 from cable needle.

Back:
With larger needles and 1 strand of wool in each color, cast on 129 (137, 145) sts and work in k1, p1 rib for 8 rows. Then work pattern as follows:

Row 1: Sl 1, rib 9, p19 (21, 23), k16, p39 (43, 47), k16, p19 (21, 23), rib 9, k1 tbl.
Row 2: Sl 1, rib 9, k19 (21, 23), p16, k39 (43, 47), p16, k19 (21, 23), rib 9, k1 tbl.

Repeat these 2 rows until 7th row and then work as follows: Sl 1, rib 9, p19 (21, 23), C16, p39 (43, 47), C16, k19 (21, 23), rib 9, k1 tbl. Cont in pattern as established and cable every 11th row, *at the same time* dec 1 st on purl bands every 13th row 4 times. Dec row will be worked as follows:
Sl 1, rib 9, p2tog, pattern to last 12 sts, p2tog, rib 9, k1 tbl. Cont in pattern on rem 121 (129, 137) sts until back measures 30 (31, 32)" / 76 (79, 81)cm from beg. End with right side facing.

Shape Shoulders:
Bind off 44 (47, 51) sts at beg of next 2 rows, binding off in pattern and k2tog across 16 cable sts. Place rem 33 (35, 35) sts on holder for neckband.

Pocket Linings: (2)
With larger needles and one strand of wool in each color, cast on 26 sts and work in rev st st (right side purl) until piece measures 6" (15cm) from beg. Place sts on holder.

Left Front:
With larger needles and one strand of wool in each color, cast on 75 (79, 83) sts and work in k1, p1 rib for 8 rows. Then beg pattern as follows:

Row 1: Sl 1, rib 9, p19 (21, 23), k16, p20 (22, 24), rib 9, k1 tbl.
Row 2: Sl 1, rib 9, k20 (22, 24), p16, k19 (21, 23), rib 9, k1 tbl.

Repeat these two rows until 7th row and then work as follows: Sl 1, rib 9, p19 (21, 23), C16, p20 (22, 24), rib 9, k1 tbl. Cont in pattern as established and cable every 11th row, *at the same time* dec 1 st on purl bands every 13th row 4 times. Dec row will be worked as follows:
Sl 1, rib 9, p2tog, p17 (19, 21), k16, p18 (20, 22), p2tog, rib 9, k1 tbl.
Cont until piece measures 6" (15cm) from beg. End with right side facing.

Place Pockets:
Work 20 (21, 22) sts, sl 26 sts onto holder, pattern across 26 sts of pocket lining (rev st st side facing), pattern to end. Work evenly until piece measures 26½ (27½, 28½)" / 67 (70, 72)cm from beg. End with right side facing.

Shape Neck:
Pattern to last 12 sts and turn, place these 12 sts on holder for neckband. Working this side only, k2tog at neck edge on next row and then every other row until 44 (47, 51) sts rem. Work evenly in pattern until piece measures 30 (31, 32)" / 76 (79, 81)cm from beg. End with right side facing.

EASY ELEGANCE

Shape Shoulder:
From shoulder edge bind off in pattern, knitting 2tog over 16 cable sts.

Right Front:
Work as for left front, reversing all shaping. When piece measures 24½ (25½, 26½)" / 62 (65, 67)cm from beg make buttonhole.

Buttonhole:
With right side facing, sl 1, rib 3, bind off 3 sts, rib 3, pattern to end of row. On next row, cast on 3 sts over bound off sts.

Sleeves:
With smaller needles and one strand of wool in each color, cast on 53 (57, 61) sts and work in k1, p1 rib for 4½" (11cm), inc 52 (48, 44) sts evenly across last row, 105 sts. Change to larger needles and pattern as follows:

Row 1: Sl 1, rib 9, p34, k16, p35, rib 9, k1 tbl.
Row 2: Sl 1, rib 9, k35, p16, k34, rib 9, k1 tbl.

Repeat these 2 rows until 7th row and then work as follows:
Sl 1, rib 9, p34, C16, p35, rib 9, k1 tbl. Cont in pattern as established, cabling every 11th row. When sleeve measures 18" (46cm), end with right side facing. Bind off in pattern, knitting 2tog across 16 sts of cable.

Neckband:
Sew shoulder seams. With smaller needles, one strand of wool in each color and right side facing, rib 12 sts from right front, pick up 20 (22, 24) sts up right front, 33 (35, 35) sts from back, 20 (22, 24) sts down left front and rib 12 sts from left front, 97 (103, 107) sts. Work in k1, p1 rib for ½" (1.5cm). End with right side facing.

Make Buttonhole:
Sl 1, rib 3, bind off 3, rib to end. Next row, cast on 3 sts over bound off sts. Work in rib until neckband measures 3¼" (8cm). End with right side facing. Make another buttonhole. Work ½" (1.5cm) more in rib. Bind off in rib.

Pocket Tops:
With smaller needles and one strand of wool in each color, pick up 26 sts from pocket and work in k1, p1 rib for 6 rows. Bind off in rib.

Finishing:
Sew in sleeves, placing center of sleeve cable to shoulder seam. Sew side and sleeve seams. Sew pocket linings and tops in place. Fold neckband in half to inside and slipstitch in place. Sew on buttons.

CHECK-MATE

This short check jacket is made in bulky Shetland yarn, knitted loosely, making it light—yet wearable and warm. It is really cozy and very striking. It's also nice and quick to knit!

Sizes:
This jacket is a "boxy" style, fairly short and wide, and should be worn loosely. Directions are for medium with large in parentheses. Finished bust measurements 40 (42)" / 102 (106)cm; both are 23" (58.5cm) long.

Materials:
15 (16) 50gm balls of Shetland bulky in MC
4 50 gm balls Shetland chunky in each CC
6 buttons

Needles:
One pair each size 9 (6mm), size 7 (5mm) and size 10½ (7mm) knitting needles, or size needed to obtain gauge.

Gauge:
8 sts = 2" (5cm) on #10½ (7mm) needles in st st.

Back:
With #9 (6mm) needles, and MC, cast on 80 (88) sts and work in k1, p1 rib for 6 rows. Change to #10½ (7mm) needles and in st st, work pattern from chart until piece measures 14" (36cm) from beg. End with right side facing.

Shape Armholes:
Bind off 8 sts at beg of next 2 rows. Allowing for bound off sts, cont working pattern from chart until piece measures 23" (58.5cm) from beg. End with right side facing.

Shape Shoulders:
Bind off 16 (18) sts at beg of next 2 rows. Place rem 32 (36) sts onto holder for neckband.

Left Front:
With #9 (6mm) needles and MC, cast on 40 (44) sts and work in k1, p1 rib for 6 rows. Change to #10½ (7mm) needles and in st st work pattern from right half of chart until piece measures 14" (36cm) from beg. (NOTE: If required length has not been reached by end of chart, repeat from row 1.) End with right side facing.

Shape Armhole:
Bind off 8 sts at beg of next row. Cont to work from chart until piece measures 19" (48cm) from beg. End with wrong side facing.

Shape Neck:
Bind off 4 sts at beg of next row, then dec 1 st at neck edge every row until 16 (18) sts rem. Work evenly until piece measures same as back to shoulder. End with right side facing.

Shape Shoulder:
Bind off 16 (18) sts at beg of next row.

Right Front:
Work as for left front, working pattern from left hand side of chart and reversing all shaping.

Sleeves:
With #7 (5mm) needles and MC, cast on 36 sts and work in k1, p1 rib for 2" (5cm). Inc 4 sts evenly across last row, 40 sts. Change to #10½ (7mm) needles and in st st work pattern from sleeve chart, *at the same time*, inc 1 st at each end of 5th and then every 4th row until there are 62 sts. Work evenly until sleeve measures 18" (46cm) or desired length. Bind off in purl.

Left Front Band:
With #9 (6mm) needles and MC, cast on 7 sts and work in k1, p1 rib (sl 1st st and k last tbl every row) until band fits front, slightly stretched. Leave sts on holder. Sew left band onto left front. With pins mark positions for 6 buttons. Begin with 1st button ¼" (1cm) from beg. The last button will be in neckband and rem 4 are evenly spaced between.

Right Front Band:
Work as for left front band, making buttonholes to correspond with button position. Make buttonholes as follows: Sl 1, rib 1, bind off 2, rib 2, k1 tbl. Next row: Cast on 2 sts over bound off sts of previous row.

Neckband:
Sew shoulder seams. With right side facing, #9 (6mm) needles and MC, pick up 7 sts from right front band, 20 (22) sts up right front neck, 32 (36) sts from back, 20 (22) sts down left front neck and 7 sts from left front band, 86 (94) sts. Work in k1, p1 rib for 3 rows. Make buttonhole in next row. Work 2 rows. Bind off in rib.

Finishing:
Sew sleeves in by matching center sleeve to shoulder seam. Sew side and sleeve seams. Weave in all ends. Sew on buttons.

CHECK-MATE

Base = Black
X = Cream
○ = Rust

Base = Cream
X = Camel
○ = Brown

Base = Red
X = White
○ = Black

Base = Royal Blue
X = White
○ = Red

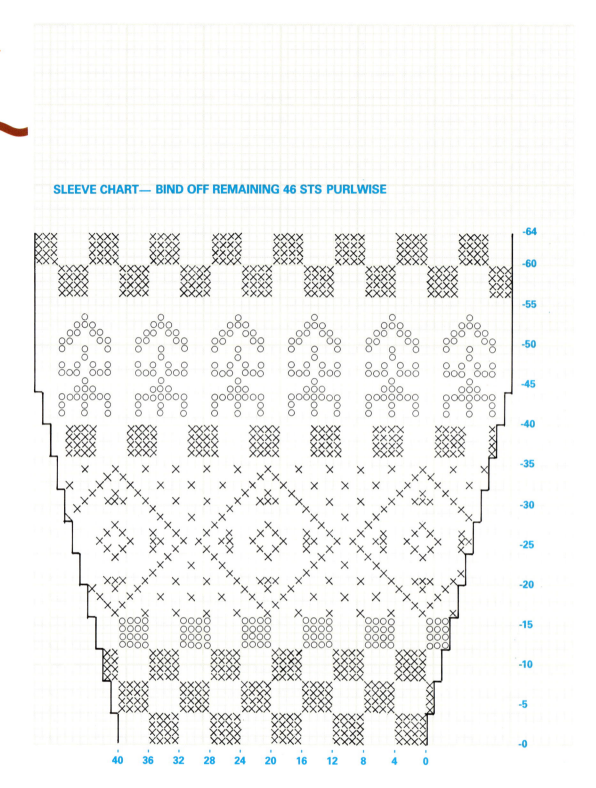

SLEEVE CHART— BIND OFF REMAINING 46 STS PURLWISE

2ND SIZE **1ST SIZE** **1ST SIZE** **2ND SIZE**

HOME
COMFORT

I was really pleased with myself when I finally finished drawing the chart for this pattern— it took me six days' solid work. When the very first sample was knitted up I was thrilled to see how well the old-fashioned letters had come out. Again, this is not easy to knit—but once done, it's a joy and a pride forever.

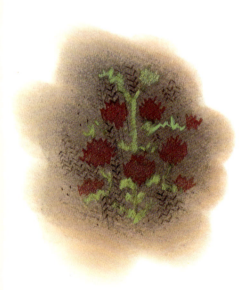

Sizes:
To fit 32 (34, 36)″ / 81 (86, 91)cm bust. Directions are for small with medium and large in parentheses.

Materials:
9 50 gram balls fingering weight Shetland wool in MC and small amounts of 8 CC
3 small buttons

Needles:
One pair each size 1 (2.50mm) and size 3 (3.25mm) knitting needles or size needed to obtain gauge.

Gauge:
13 sts and 16 rows = 2″ (5cm) on #3 (3.25mm) needles over st st.

Back:
With smaller needles and MC cast on 96 (100, 104) sts and work in k1, p1 rib for 3″ (7.5cms). Inc 12 (14,16) sts across last row, 108 (114, 120) sts. Change to larger needles and work in st st until piece measures 14″ (36cms) from beg. End with right side facing.

Shape Armholes:
Bind off 5 sts at the beg of the next 2 rows. Then dec 1 st each side every other row until 94 (98, 102) sts rem. Work evenly until piece measures 21½ (22, 22½)″ / 54.5 (56, 57)cms from beg.

Shape Shoulders:
Bind off 12 (13,14) sts at beg of next 4 rows. Place rem 46 sts on holder.

Front:
Work ribbing as for back, on last row inc 18 (20, 22) sts evenly across row, 114 (120, 126) sts. Change to larger needles and work pattern as follows: Sl 1, k2 (5, 8), work across row 1 of chart, end k2 (5, 8), k1 tbl. Cont to follow chart with 3 (6, 9) sts in MC on each side until piece measures same as back to armholes.

Shape Armholes:
Cont in pattern, bind off 5 (8, 11) sts at the beg of the next 2 rows, 104 sts. (NOTE: 2 sts either side will be taken out of the pattern in the bind off.) Work evenly until front measures 19 (19½, 20)″ / 48 (49.5, 51)cms from beg. End with right side facing.

Neck Shaping:
Work across 35 sts, turn and work this side only. Dec 1 st at neck edge every row 9 times, 26 sts. When pattern is complete work in MC until piece measures same as back to shoulder shaping.

Shape Shoulder:
Bind off 13 sts at beg of next row and then every other row once. Sl center 34 sts onto a holder for neckband. Work second side to match first, reversing all shaping.

Sleeves:
With smaller needles cast on 46 sts and work in k1, p1 ribbing for 3″ (7.5cms). Inc 10 sts evenly across last row, 56 sts. Change to larger needles and work in st st. Inc 1 st at each end of 7th row and then every 4th row until 96 sts. Work evenly until sleeve measures 18″ (46cms) from beg.

Shape Cap:
Bind off 4 sts at beg of the next 2 rows. Dec 1 st at each end of every row until 68 sts rem, then dec 1 st at each end every other row until 36 sts rem. End with right side facing. Next row: k3tog across row. Bind off.

Neckband:
Sew right shoulder seam. With smaller needles and right side facing, pick up 25 sts in MC down left side, 34 sts from center front, 25 sts up right side and 46 sts from center back. Work in k1, p1 rib for 6 rows. Bind off in rib.

Finishing:
Sew left shoulder seam, leaving 2½″ (6cm) open at neck. Line center of sleeve up with shoulder seam and sew in sleeves. Sew sleeve and side seams. Sew in all pattern ends. Sew 3 buttons on back of left shoulder opening. Crochet chain st loops to fit buttons.

HOME COMFORT

× = Wine
| = Red
▽ = Rust
○ = Gold
● = Brown
◢ = Moss Green
■ = Bottle Green
◇ = Pilot Blue

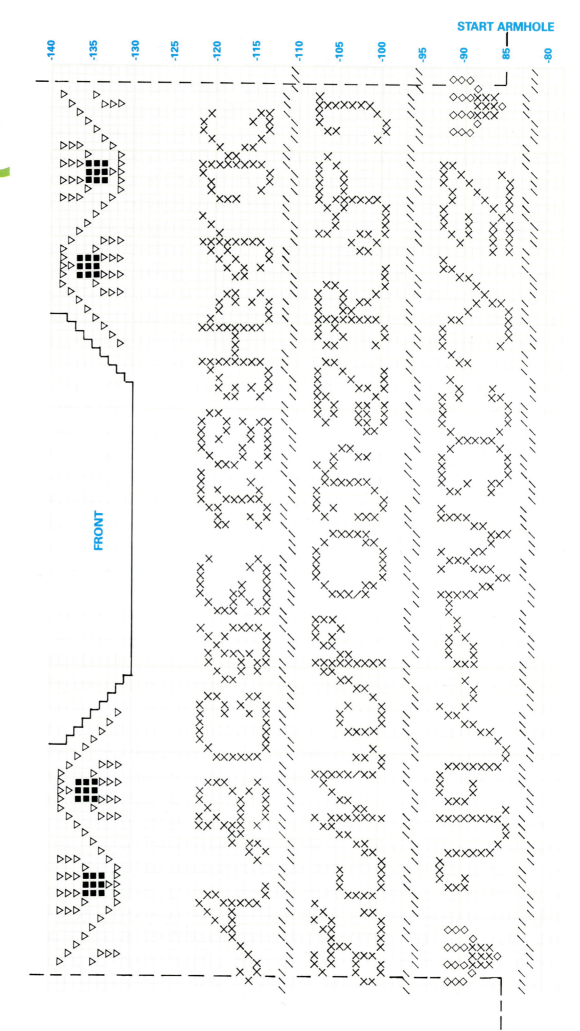

START ARMHOLE

FRONT

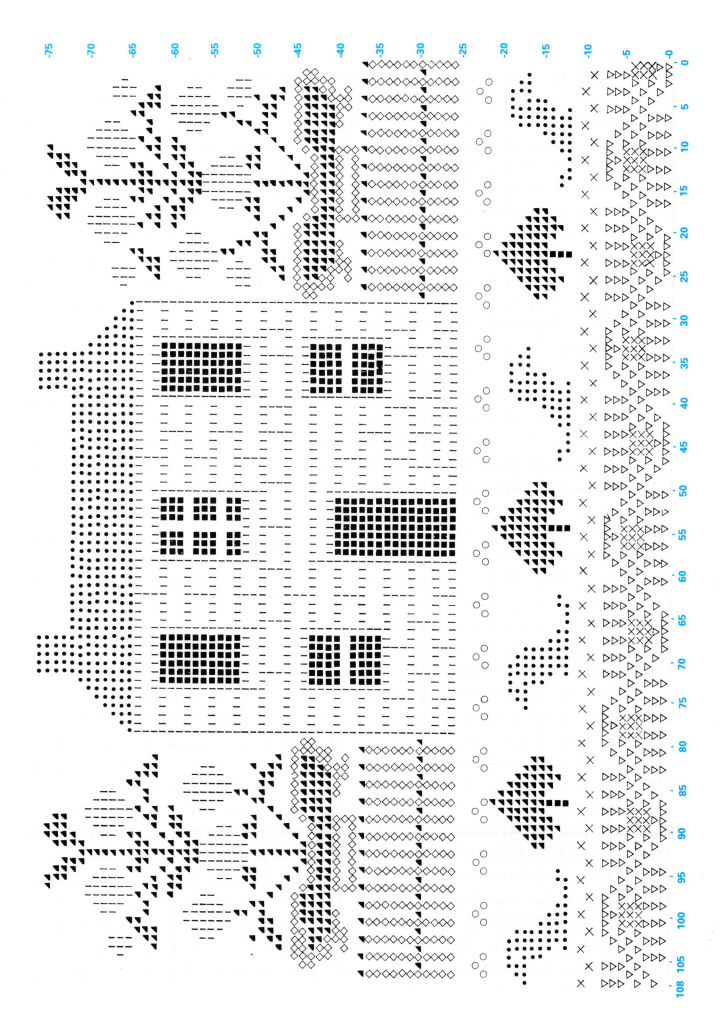

FLOWER POWER

This one has sold very well all over the world. A sweater with punch and impact, it's colorful and exciting to wear—a super look with a loose and easy fit.

Sizes:
One size. Oversized sweater that measures 48″ (122cm) across bust.

Materials:
10 50 gm balls of worsted weight in MC
1 50 gm ball of each of the 4 CC

Needles:
One pair each size 3 (3.25mm) and size 7 (4.50mm) knitting needles or size needed to obtain gauge.

Gauge:
10 sts = 2″ (5cm) on #7 (5mm) needles over st st.

Note:
Use yarn bobbins for pattern to avoid tangles. *Do not carry MC across back of floral pattern*; use separate balls on each side of pattern. *Always* twist yarn when changing color to avoid holes in fabric.

Back:
With smaller needles and MC, cast on 120 sts and work in k1, p1 rib for 2½″ (6cm). Change to larger needles and work chart A for back, until chart is completed (170 rows).

Shape Shoulders:
Bind off 38 sts at the beg of the next 2 rows. Place rem 44 sts onto a holder for neckband.

Front:
Work rib as for back. Change to larger needles and follow chart B for front.

Neck Shaping:
On 147th row (see chart B) beg neck shaping. Work across 49 sts and turn. Following the chart and working this side only, dec 1 st on neck edge every row until 38 sts rem. Work evenly until chart B is completed. Bind off 38 sts for shoulder. Sl 22 center sts onto a holder for neckband. Join yarn to rem 49 sts and work to correspond to first side, reversing all shaping.

Sleeves:
With smaller needles and MC, cast on 44 sts and work in k1, p1 rib for 3″ (7.5cm). Inc 36 sts evenly spaced across last row, 80 sts. Change to larger needles and work in st st. Inc 1 st each side of 5th row and then every 4th row 8 times, 100 sts. *At the same time*, when sleeve measures 8″ (20cm) from beg, follow chart C for sleeve. (NOTE: If you have not reached 100 sts when sleeve chart starts, just place pattern centrally.) When chart C is complete, bind off.

Neckband:
Join right shoulder seam. With smaller needles and right side facing, beg at left shoulder and pick up 22 sts down left side, 22 sts from center front, 22 sts up right side and 44 sts from back. Work in k1, p1 rib for 8 rows. Bind off loosely in rib. Join left shoulder seam.

Finishing:
Pin center sleeve to shoulder seam. Measure and pin sleeve edge, making sure the armhole length is the same each side of the shoulder seam. Sew into place. Sew side and sleeve seams. Sew in all ends.

FLOWER POWER

CHART A
BACK CHART

BACK(A) AND SLEEVE(C) CHART

FOLLOW SLEEVE
INSTRUCTIONS UP
TO 8" (20cm). IF YOU HAVE
NOT REACHED 100 STS
WHEN SLEEVE CHART
STARTS JUST SET
IT CENTRALLY.

BIND OFF ON
74TH ROW

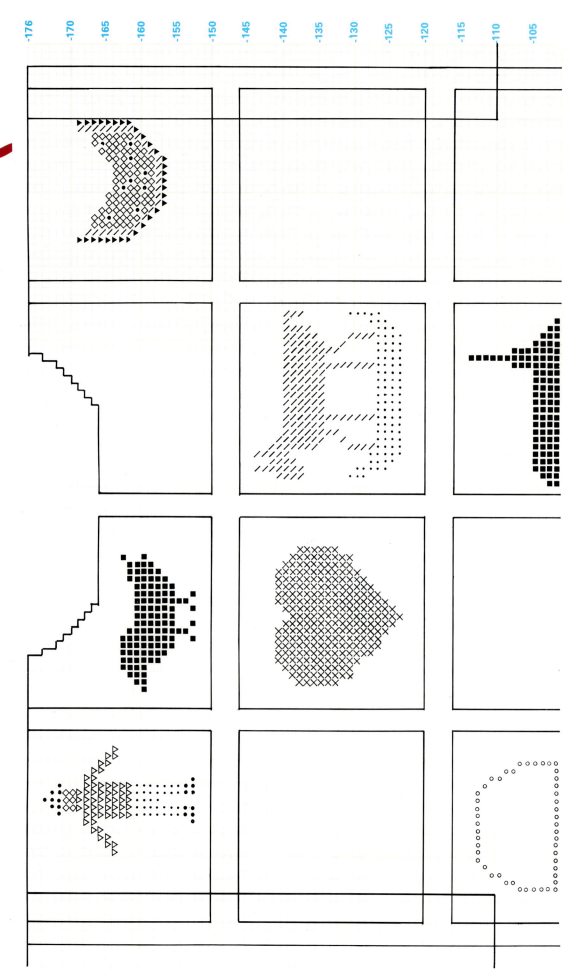

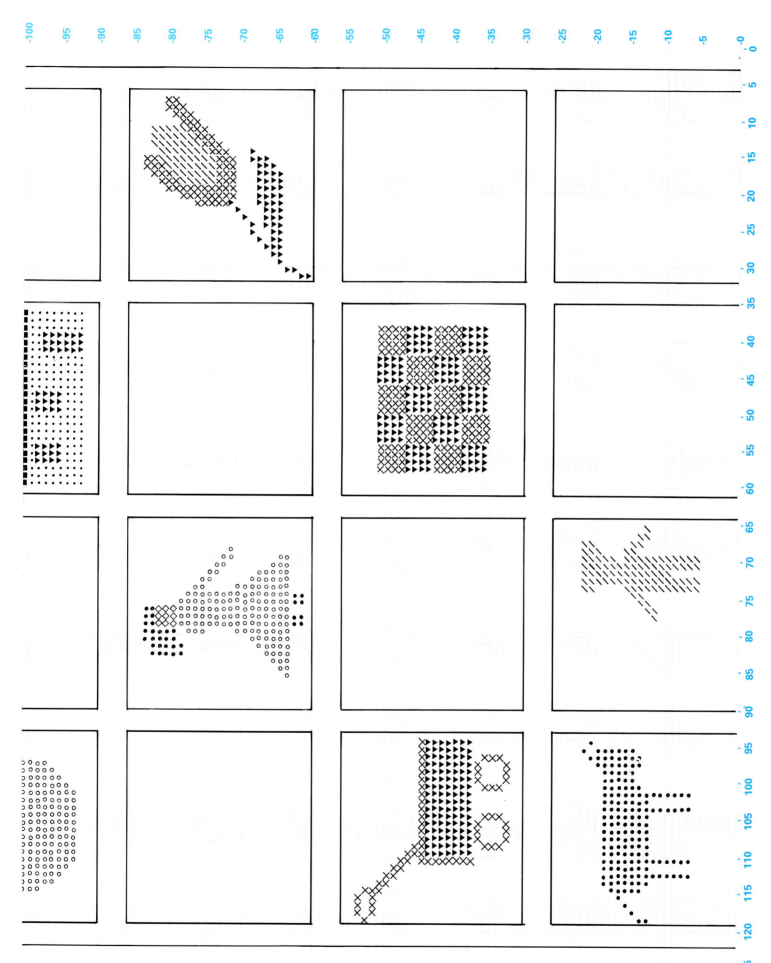

VESTED INTEREST

This patchwork slipover vest is a popular favorite. It is such an asset to a wardrobe as it can be worn with casuals or with soft skirts and blouses and lace.

The design is also very versatile; you can use the basic pattern and draw in your own motifs. I have done a variety of themes, like holidays and the 12 days of Christmas.

Sizes:
To fit 32/34 (34/36)″ / 81/86 (86/91)cm bust sizes. Directions are for small with medium in parentheses.

Materials:
5 50 gm balls of fingering weight Shetland wool in MC
Small amounts of 11 CC (wine, cream, red, pink, mauve, gold, black, pilot blue, bottle green, chocolate, pink)

Needles:
One pair size 3 (3.25mm). For larger size, size 4 (3.50mm) or size needed to obtain gauge.

Gauge:
14 sts and 16 rows = 2″ (5cm) square on #3 (3.25mm) needles over st st.

Back & Front:
With #3 (#4) / 3.25mm (3.50mm) needles and MC, cast on 100 sts and work in single seed st (Row 1: k1, p1 rep across row. Row 2: p the k sts and k the p sts of previous row) for 1½″ (4cm). Inc 19 sts evenly spaced across last row, 119 sts. Knit 3 rows. (NOTE: The body of the sweater is divided into garter st squares. Each motif is 26 sts X 26 rows. Some of the squares are plain, some have motifs. Consult chart.)

Next row: K3, * p26, k3, rep from * to end.
Next row: Knit.
These last two rows are rep 13 times, knitting in motifs where relevant. When motifs are complete, knit 4 rows. This completes the first row of squares. Cont with pattern as set until row 20 of the 4th row of squares.

Armband:
Work the first 7 and the last 7 sts in seed st for armbands. Cont working 7 sts each side in seed st every row. Work evenly until 16th row of last set of squares.

Neck Shaping:
Work across 7 seed sts, 39 pattern sts and turn, work this side only. Dec 1 st each side of neck edge every row 6 times, 33 patt sts. Then dec 1 st at neck edge every other row once, 39 sts. Work 1 row. Bind off 39 sts from shoulder edge. Return to rem sts and place center 27 sts onto holder for neck. Join yarn to rem sts and work to match first side, reversing all shaping.

Neckband:
Join right shoulder seam. With #3 (3.25mm) needles, MC and right side facing, pick up 15 sts down left front, 27 sts across center front, 29 sts up right neckline and 27 sts across back, 14 sts left back neckline, 112 sts. Work in single seed st for 5 rows. Bind off *loosely* in seed st.

Finishing:
Sew in all ends. Join left shoulder seam. Sew side seams below seed st armbands, being careful to match up squares.

-170 -165 -160 -155 -150 -145 -140 -135 -130 -125 -120 -115 -110 -105 -100

CHART B
FRONT CHART

WINTER WARMER

A very comforting addition to any man or woman's wardrobe, this sweater's snug turtleneck and understated appeal will help you get through those cold winter days in style.

Sizes:
To fit up to 36″ (91cm) and 40″ (102cm) bust. Directions are for small with medium in parentheses.

Materials:
13 50 gm balls of Aran weight wool

Needles:
One pair each size 3 (3.25mm), size 4 (3.50mm) and size 7 (5mm) knitting needles or size needed to obtain gauge.

Gauge:
9 sts = 2″ (5cm) on #7 (5mm) needles over st st

Back:
With #3 (3.25mm) needles cast on 84 (90) sts and work in k1, p1 rib for 3″ (7.5cm). Inc in last row as follows: rib 2 (5), inc in every other st to last 2 (5) then rib, 124 (130) sts. Change to #7 (5mm) needles and pattern as follows:

Row 1: Sl 1, k0 (3), (p1, k1, p1, k6, p1, k1, p1, k10) 5 times, p1, k1, p1, k6, p1, k1, p1, k0 (3), k1 tbl.
Row 2: Sl 1, p0 (3), k1, p1, k1, p6, k1, p1, k1, (p10, k1, p1, k1, p6, k1, p1, k1) 5 times, p0 (3), k1 tbl.
Row 3: Work as for row 1 but work cable 6f instead of k6. (C6f = Cable 6f = sl next 3 sts onto a cable needle and leave at front of work, k3, then k3 from cable needle.)
Row 4: Work as for row 2.
Row 5: Work as for row 1.
Row 6: Work as for row 2.
Row 7: Work as for row 3 and also cable 10 back instead of k10 (C10b = Cable 10 back = sl next 5 sts onto cable needle and hold in back of work, k5, then k5 from cable needle.)

Row 8: Work as for row 2.

These 8 rows form the pattern. Repeat these 8 rows until piece measures 16 (16½)″ / 40.5 (42)cm.

Shape Armholes:
Bind off 7 (9) sts at beg of next 2 rows, working 2 sts tog across cable panel (actually losing 10 (11) sts). Next row: k2tog tbl at each end of row *for medium size*; work 3 sts tog at each end. Armhole shaping is complete for small size. For medium size only: on next row, k2tog, work to last 2 sts, k2tog tbl. For both sizes work evenly on 102 sts in pattern until piece measures 24 (24½)″ / 61 (62)cm from beg.

Shape Shoulders:
Bind off 10 sts at beg of next 2 rows, working 2 sts tog across cable panel (actually losing 15 sts). Bind off 11 sts at beg of next 2 rows (actually losing 19 sts). Sl rem 34 sts onto holder for neck.

Front:
Work as for back until piece measures 22½ (23)″ / 57 (58.5)cm from beg. End with right side facing. Work across 43 sts, turn and work back. Working this side only dec 1 st at neck edge every row 4 times, then every other row until 34 sts rem. Work evenly until piece measures same as back to shoulder. End at side edge.

Shape Shoulder:
Bind off 10 sts at beg of next row, working 2 sts tog across cable panel (actually losing 15 sts). Work 1 row. Bind off 11 sts at beg of next row (actually losing 19 sts). Sl center 16 sts onto a holder for neck. Join yarn and work to correspond to first side, reversing all shaping.

Sleeves:
With #3 (3.25mm) needles cast on 40 sts and work in k1, p1 rib for 3″ (7.5cm). Inc in every st across last row, 80 sts. Change to #7 (5mm) needles and work in pattern as follows:

WINTER WARMER

Row 1: Sl 1, (p1, k1, p1, k6, p1, k1, p1, k10) 3 times, p1, k1, p1, k6, p1, k1, p1, k1 tbl.
Row 2: Sl 1, (k1, p1, k1, p6, k1, p1, k1, p10) 3 times, k1, p1, k1, p6, k1, p1, k1, k1 tbl.
Row 3: Work as for row 1 but C6f instead of k6.
Row 4: Work as for row 2.
Row 5: Work as for row 1.
Row 6: Work as for row 2.
Row 7: Work as for row 3 but C10b instead of k10.
Row 8: Work as for row 2.

Repeat these 8 rows for pattern, *at the same time* inc 1 st at each end of next row and then every 8th row until 98 sts. (NOTE: Work all inc sts in k1, p1 rib.) Work evenly until piece measures 18″ (46cm), or desired length to underarm.

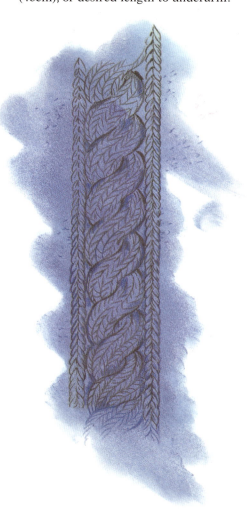

Shape Cap:
Bind off 4 sts at beg of next 4 rows, then dec 1 st at each end of every other row (k3tog across all cables) 15 times (30 rows). End with right side facing. K3tog across next row. Bind off rem sts.

Turtleneck:
Sew right shoulder seam. With right side facing and #4 (3.50mm) needles pick up 28 sts down left front, 16 sts from center front, 28 sts up right front, 34 sts from back. Work in k1, p1 rib for 3″ (7.5cm). Dec 4 sts evenly across last row, 102 sts. Change to #7 (5mm) needles and with *wrong* side facing work in pattern as for sleeve, repeating pattern in parentheses 4 times instead of 3; substitute C6 back instead of C6f and instead of C10 back do C10 front (this will continue cable pattern to other side). Work in pattern for 4″ (10cm). End with right side facing. Next row: Rib 4, * (k2tog, p2tog, rib 7, p2tog, k2tog, rib 7), rep from * to end. Work 6 rows in k1, p1 rib. Bind off loosely in rib.

Finishing:
Sew left shoulder seam. Sew sleeves into place. Sew side and sleeve seams.
NOTE: Avoid blocking as it will flatten cables.

COLD STAND-ARDS

Combining the well-loved cable with the very popular basket stitch, this is a man's favorite, made in heathery Shetland yarn. Easily worn by a woman, too!

Sizes:
For medium, up to 40″ (102cm), use #5 (4mm) needles; for larger size, up to 44″ (112cm) use #7 (5mm) needles.

Materials:
11 50 gm balls Shetland sportweight yarn

Needles:
One pair each size 2 (3mm) and size 5 (4mm) or size 7 (5mm) knitting needles, or size needed to obtain gauge.

Gauge:
11 sts = 2″ (5cm) on #5 (4mm) needles over st st. For larger size, 10 sts = 2″ (5cm) on #7 (5mm) needles over st st.

Back:
With smaller needles, cast on 122 sts and work in k1, p1 rib for 3½″ (9cm). Next row: Rib 6, (inc into next st, rib 11) 9 times, inc into next st, rib to end, 132 sts. Change to larger needles and work in cable and basket pattern as follows:

Row 1: * K4, p4, k4, p2, k8, p2. Repeat from * 5 times, k4, p4, k4.
Row 2: * P4, k4, p4, k2, p8, k2. Repeat from * 5 times, p4, k4, p4.
Row 3: Work as for row 1.
Row 4: Work as for row 2.
Row 5: * P4, k4, p4, p2, C4 (C4 = Cable 4 = sl 4 sts onto cable needle and hold at front of work, k4, k4 from cable needle), p2. Repeat from * 5 times p4, k4, p4.
Row 6: * K4, p4, k4, k2, p8, k2. Repeat from * 5 times, k4, p4, k4.
Row 7: * P4, k4, p4, p2, k8, p2. Repeat from * 5 times, p4, k4, p4.
Row 8: Work as for row 6.

These 8 rows form pattern which is repeated throughout. Cont in pattern until piece measures 17½″ (44.5cm) from beg. End with right side facing.

Shape Armholes:
Bind off 8 sts at beg of next 2 rows. Then, dec 1 st at each end of every other row 4 times, 108 sts. Cont in pattern and work evenly until piece measures 27″ (68.5cm) from beg. End with right side facing.

Shape Shoulder:
Bind off 16 sts at beg of next 4 rows. Place rem 44 sts on holder for neckband.

Front:
Work as for back until front measures 16″ (40.5cm) from beg. End with right side facing. Divide for "V" as follows: Pattern across 66 sts and turn. Working this side only, dec 1 st at neck edge on next row and then every 4th row until piece measures same as back to armhole, 17½″ (44.5cm).

Shape Armholes:
Bind off 8 sts at beg of next armhole edge, then dec 1 st at armhole edge every other row 4 times. Dec at neck edge every 4th row until 32 sts rem. Work evenly on these 32 sts until piece measures same as back to shoulder.

Shape Shoulder:
Bind off 16 sts at beg of next row, then every other row once. Join yarn to rem 66 sts and work to match first side, reversing all shaping.

Cold Stand- ards

Sleeves:

With smaller needles, cast on 60 sts and work in k1, p1 rib for 3″ (7.5cm). Next row: Rib 8, (inc into next st, rib 2) 15 times, inc into next st, rib to end, 76 sts. Change to larger needles and pattern as follows:

Row 1: P4, k4, * p2, k8, p2, k4, p4, k4. Repeat from * once more, p2, k8, p2, k4, p4.
Row 2: K4, p4, * k2, p8, k2, p4, k4, p4. Repeat from * once more, k2, p8, k2, p4, k4.
Row 3: Work as for row 1.
Row 4: Work as for row 2.
Row 5: K4, p4, * p2, C4, p2, p4, k4, p4. Repeat from * once more, p2, C4, p2, p4, k4.
Row 6: P4, k4, * k2, p8, k2, k4, p4, k4. Repeat from * once more, k2, p8, k2, k4, p4.

Row 7: K4, p4, * p2, k8, p2, p4, k4, p4. Repeat from * once more, p2, k8, p2, p4, k4.
Row 8: Work as for row 6.

Cont in pattern, inc 1 st at each end of 11th row and then every 8th row until there are 98 sts, work all inc sts into basket st. Work evenly until sleeve measures 18½″ (47cm) from beg. End with right side facing.

Shape Cap:

Bind off 8 sts at beg of next 2 rows, then dec 1 st at each end of every row 18 times, 46 sts rem. Work 1 row. Bind off 6 sts at beg of next 6 rows. Bind off rem 10 sts.

Neckband:

Join right shoulder seam. With smaller needles and right side facing, beg at left shoulder and pick up 80 sts down left side of neck, inc 1 st by picking up and knitting into the back of the center loop (mark this st), 80 sts up right side of neck and 44 sts from center back, 205 sts. Work 10 rows in k1, p1 rib, *at the same time* k2tog at each side of center st every row. Bind off in rib.

Finishing:

Sew left shoulder seam. Set sleeves into armholes and sew side and sleeve seams.

Sporting Specials

This section includes ski sweaters and a group of fabulous Fair Isles. Sweaters like these have had a strong impact on high fashion, bringing handknits right to the forefront, where I am sure they will stay. ■ The couture houses have come to appreciate the difference and individual beauty of a handknitted garment. The variations in texture and stitch reflect each knitter's personality and interpretation, giving each garment truly unique qualities. No machine, however sophisticated, will ever produce the same "handle." ■ For the sweaters with motifs, see the hints given with regard to the sampler sweaters in "Country Casuals." Don't forget that motifs can be swapped round and colors changed. To me, color is the most exciting part of designing—experimenting with families of color, soft tones, rich tones, and sometimes a really heterogeneous array. Never be afraid to mix what may seem unusual—think of a garden!

SKI TEAM
—His & Hers

Super to wear either on or off the slopes. These two sweaters depict ski motifs for men and women combined with a simple but effective Fair Isle yoke. The women's style has the added interest of motifs on the sleeves. Made in warm bulky yarn, they bring the panache of the piste to your wardrobe.

Sizes:
To fit 36 (40, 44)″ / 91 (102, 112)cm chest. (Woman's sweater is worn loosely.) Directions are for small with medium and large in parentheses.

Materials:
18 50 gm balls of Shetland bulky in MC
Small amounts of 8 CC

Needles:
One pair each size 5 (4mm) and size 8 (5.5mm) knitting needles, or size needed to obtain gauge.

Gauge:
15 sts and 22 rows = 4″ (10cm) over st st on #8 (5.5mm) needles.

Note:
Always twist yarns around each other when changing colors to avoid holes in fabric.

Front:
With smaller needles and MC, cast on 68 (76, 84) sts and work in k1, p1 rib for 3″ (7.5cm). Change to larger needles and work 4 rows in st st. Work either chart A or chart B for front pattern. Set chart as follows: k3 (7, 11), work across 62 sts of 1st row of chart, k to end. Cont to work in chart until complete, then work in MC until piece measures 18″ (46cm) from beg. End with right side facing.

Shape Armholes:
Bind off 4 sts at beg of next 2 rows. Work evenly for 7 rows. On the 8th row inc 4sts evenly across row, 64 (72, 80) sts. Follow chart C for Fair Isle pattern. On 18th row of pattern begin neck shaping.

Neck Shaping:
Work across 24 (28, 32) sts and turn. Working this side only, dec 1 st at neck edge every row 8 times, 16 (20, 24) sts. Cont in pattern until complete. Work in MC (if necessary) until piece measures 26½ (26½, 27½)″ / 67 (67, 70)cm from beg. End at side edge.

Shape Shoulders:
Bind off 8 (10, 12) sts on shoulder edge every other row twice. Return to rem sts and sl center 16 sts onto holder for neck. Join yarn and work to match first side, reversing all shaping.

Back:
Work as for front, omitting chart A/B but including chart C (Fair Isle). Work chart C without the neckline shaping. Cont evenly until back measures same as front to shoulders.

Shape Shoulders:
Bind off 8 (10, 12) sts at beg of next 4 rows. Place rem 32 sts onto holder.

Sleeves:
With smaller needles and MC, cast on 40 sts and work in k1, p1 rib for 3″ (7.5cm). Inc 8 sts evenly across last row, 48 sts. Change to larger needles and work rows 1–10 from chart C. Then in MC inc 1 st at each side of next row, repeat inc every 6th row until there are 62 sts. Work evenly until sleeve measures 19″ (48cm) from beg.

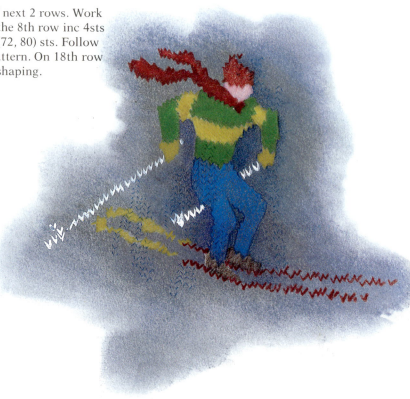

S KI
T EAM

Shape Cap:

Bind off 3 sts at beg of next 2 rows. Beg with next row, dec 1 st at each end of every other row 4 times, 48 sts. End with right side facing. Beg chart D, cont to dec every other row. When chart is complete work 1 row in MC. Bind off in next row.

Neckband:

Sew left shoulder seam. With smaller needles, MC and right side facing, pick up 18 sts down left front of neck, 16 sts from center front, 18 sts up right front of sweater, 32 sts from back, 84 sts. Work k1, p1 rib for 1" (2.5cm). Bind off in rib.

Finishing:

Sew left shoulder seam. Sew in all ends. Set sleeves into armholes, matching up Fair Isle pattern. Sew side and sleeve seams.

Alternative Designs For Sleeves:

Left Sleeve: (Alternative)

Work as for left sleeve until 9th row after first Fair Isle band, then work across 10 sts, work across 30 sts of row 1 of chart E, work to end. With pattern set, work up chart and then cont in MC only and complete sleeve as indicated.

Right Sleeve:

Work as for left sleeve setting chart F when there are 56 sts on needle. Work as follows: K7, work across 42 sts of chart F, k7. When chart is complete finish sleeve as indicated.

S KI T EAM
—H IS & H ERS

CHART A

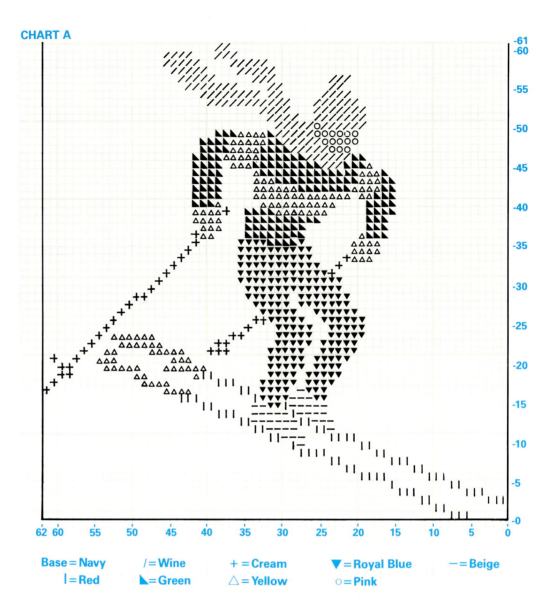

-61
-60
-55
-50
-45
-40
-35
-30
-25
-20
-15
-10
-5
-0

62 60   55   50   45   40   35   30   25   20   15   10   5   0

Base = Navy   **/ = Wine**   **+ = Cream**   **▼ = Royal Blue**   **— = Beige**

| = Red   **◣ = Green**   **△ = Yellow**   **○ = Pink**

CHART E

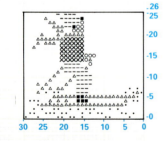

-26
-25
-20
-15
-10
-5
-0

30   25   20   15   10   5   0

CHART F

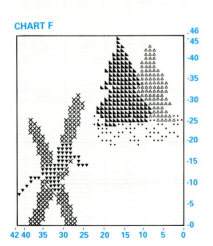

-46
-45
-40
-35
-30
-25
-20
-15
-10
-5
-0

42 40   35   30   25   20   15   10   5   0

CHART C—BACK/FRONT (FOLLOW DARK NECKLINE FOR FRONT) FAIR ISLE YOKE

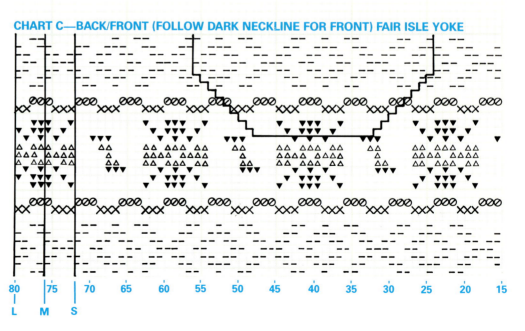

80   75   70   65   60   55   50   45   40   35   30   25   20   15

L   M   S

CHART B

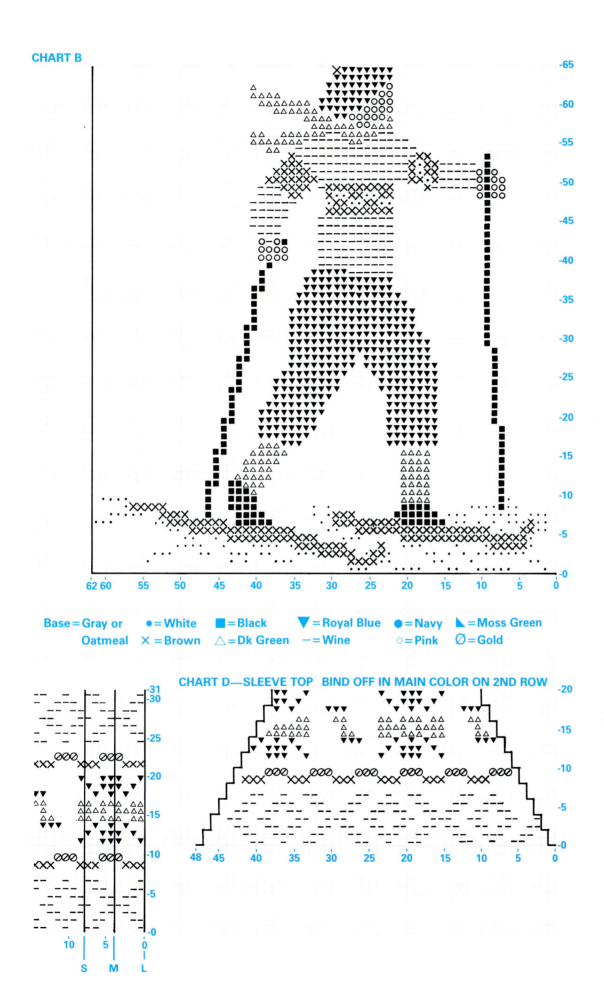

62 60 55 50 45 40 35 30 25 20 15 10 5 0

-65
-60
-55
-50
-45
-40
-35
-30
-25
-20
-15
-10
-5
-0

Base = Gray or • = White   ■ = Black   ▼ = Royal Blue   ● = Navy   ◣ = Moss Green
Oatmeal   ✕ = Brown   △ = Dk Green   — = Wine   ○ = Pink   Ø = Gold

CHART D—SLEEVE TOP   BIND OFF IN MAIN COLOR ON 2ND ROW

-31
-30
-25
-20
-15
-10
-5
-0

10   5   0
S   M   L

48   45   40   35   30   25   20   15   10   5   0

-20
-15
-10
-5
-0

SLEIGH BELLE

This is another of my special favorites, with its flattering high turtleneck, gorgeous colors, and extra-special motifs. It is made in sportweight yarn and is figure-hugging and cozy.

Sizes:
To fit 34 (36, 38)"/86 (91, 96)cm bust. Directions are for small size with medium and large in parentheses.

Materials:
14 50 gram balls of sportweight yarn in MC
Small quantities of 12 CC

Needles:
One pair each size 2 (3mm) and size 5 (4mm) knitting needles, or size needed to obtain gauge.

Gauge:
24 sts and 28 rows = 4" (10cm) on #5 needles over st st.

Front:
With smaller needles and MC, cast on 90 (98, 104) sts and work in k2, p2 rib for 3" (7.5cm). Inc 10 sts evenly across last row, 100 (108, 114) sts. Change to larger needles and work 12 rows in st st. Then set chart A as follows:

Row 1: Sl 1, k6 (10, 13), work 86 sts of first row of chart, k6 (10, 13) k1 tbl.
Row 2: Sl 1, p6 (10, 13), work 86 sts of second row of chart, p6 (10, 13), k1 tbl.

With chart set, work up chart until piece measures 13½ (14, 14½)" / 34 (36, 37)cm from cast on edge. End with right side facing.

Shape Armholes:
Bind off 6 sts at beg of next 2 rows, then dec 1 st at each end of every other row until 82 (90, 96) sts rem. (NOTE: small size will be minus 2 sts either side from chart.) Work evenly until piece measures 20½ (21, 21½)" / 52 (53, 54.5)cm from cast on edge. End with right side facing. (Work in MC when chart is complete.)

Shape Neck:
Work across 28 (32, 35) sts and turn. Working this side only, dec 1 st on neck edge every row until 22 (24, 26) sts rem. Work evenly until piece measures 22 (22½, 23)" / 56 (57, 58.5)cms from cast on edge. End at shoulder edge.

Shape Shoulder:
Bind off 11 (12, 13) sts at beg of next and every other row, once. Return to rem sts and sl center 26 sts onto holder for neck. Join yarn and work to match first side, reversing all shaping.

Back:
Work in ribbing as for front. Change to larger needles and work in st st for 8 rows. Then set chart B as follows: Sl 1, k6, work 40 sts from chart, k to end. When chart is completed, work in MC until back measures same as front to armhole.

Shape Armholes:
Bind off 6 sts at beg of next 2 rows, then dec 1 st at each end of every other row until 82 (90, 96) sts rem. Work evenly until piece measures same as front to shoulder. End with right side facing.

Sleigh Belle

Shape Shoulders:

Bind off 11 (12, 13) sts at beg of next 4 rows. Leave rem 38 (42, 44) sts on holder for neckband.

Left Sleeve:

With smaller needles and MC, cast on 46 sts and work in k2, p2 rib for 3″ (7.5cm). Inc 10 sts evenly across last row, 56 sts. Change to larger needles and work in st st, inc 1 st at each end of 5th row and then every 4th row, 12 times (80 sts). *At the same time*, when the first 12 rows of st st have been completed set chart E as follows: k26, work across 16 sts of first row of chart, k to end. When chart is finished work in MC. Work evenly until sleeve measures 18″ (46cm) from cast on edge.

Shape Cap:

Bind off 5 sts at beg of next 2 rows, then dec 1 st at each end of every row 5 times. Then dec 1 st each side every other row, until sleeve measures 23½″ (60cm) from cast on edge. Working 2 sts tog bind off.

Right Sleeve:

Work as for left sleeve, working chart C in place of chart E, setting chart as follows: k10, work across 39 sts of first row of chart, k to end. Cont to inc every 4th row, and when chart is finished work in MC until there are 80 sts on needle. Then set chart D as follows: k26, work 22 sts from chart, k to end. Complete as for left sleeve.

Turtleneck:

Sew right shoulder seam. With right side facing, smaller needles and MC, pick up 16 sts evenly down left front, 26 sts from center front, 16 sts up right front, and 38 (42, 44) sts from back. Work in k2, p2 rib for 8″ (20cm). Bind off *loosely* in rib. (NOTE: You may wish to use one needle size larger for the bind off.)

Finishing:

Sew left shoulder and turtleneck seam, sewing last 4″ (10cm) of turtleneck on right side. Set sleeves in armholes and sew into place. Sew in all ends. Sew side and sleeve seams.

SLEIGH BELLE

Base = Blue/Purple
◣ = ◇ = **Pale Blue**
● = **White**
▽ = **Dk Blue**
● = **Dk Brown**

\+ = **Taupe (Dk Beige)**
| = **Red**
■ = **Bottle (Dk Green)**
▲ = **Moss (Mid Green)**

△ = **Farn (Lt Green)**
○ = **Pink**
× = **Black**
Ø = **Gold**

CHART B—BACK TREES

CHART C—RIGHT SLEEVE

**CHART E—
LEFT SLEEVE**

CHART D—RIGHT SLEEVE

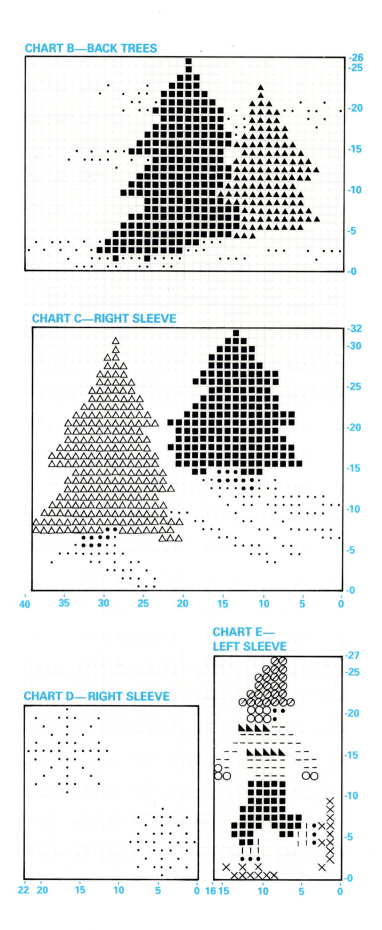

THE HUNTSMAN

This hunting scene motif is enormously popular. A simply styled jacket knit with 2 strands of fingering weight yarn—either wool or cotton—it appeals to both classical and sporty markets.

Sizes:
To fit 42 (44, 46)" / 102 (112, 117)cm chest. May be worn as a loose fitting woman's jacket. Directions are for small with medium and large in parentheses.

Materials:
22 50 gm balls of fingering weight yarn in MC
1 50 gm ball in first CC
small amounts in 6 colors
5 buttons

Needles:
One pair each size 7 (4.50mm) and size 9 (5.50mm) knitting needles or size needed to obtain gauge.

Gauge:
17 sts = 4" (10cm) with 2 strands of fingering weight wool on #9 (5.50mm) needles over st st.

Back:
With smaller needles, 2 strands of MC, cast on 98 (100, 102) sts and work in k1, p1 rib for 2½" (6cm). Change to larger needles and work in st st until piece measures 11½" (29cm). End with right side facing. Beg row 1 of chart A, as indicated for chosen size. Work chart until it is completed. Then cont in MC until back measures 29 (29½, 29½)" / 74 (75, 75)cm from beg.

Shape Shoulders:
Bind off 12 (13, 13) sts at beg of next 6 rows. Bind off rem 26 (22, 24) sts.

Pocket Linings: (make 2)
With larger needles, 2 strands of MC, cast on 20 sts and work in st st for 5" (13cm), place sts on holder.

Left Front:
With smaller needles, 2 strands of MC, cast on 44 (46, 48) sts and work in k1, p1 rib for 2½" (6cm). Change to larger needles and work in st st until piece measures 3½" (9cm). End with right side facing. Set chart B as follows: k 10 (11, 12) sts, then work across 25 sts of first row of chart, end k9 (10, 11) sts. With chart B set, continue until chart is completed. Work in MC until piece measures 11" (28cm). End with right side facing.

Place Pocket:
K 12 (13, 14), sl next 20 sts onto holder, k across 20 sts of pocket lining, k to end of row. Work evenly until front measures 17 (18, 18)" / 43 (46, 46)cm from beg. End with wrong side facing.

Shape Neck:
Dec 1 st at beg of next row (neck edge) and then every foll 4th row until 36 (39, 39) sts rem. Work evenly until piece measures same as back to shoulder. End with right side facing.

Shape Shoulders:
Bind off 12 (13, 13) sts at beg of next row and then every other row 2 times.

Right Front:
Work as for left front until 3½" (9cm) to beg of chart. Set chart C as follows: k13 (14, 15) sts, k across 18 sts of first row of chart, end k13 (14, 15) sts. Cont to work as for left front reversing all shaping.

THE HUNTSMAN

Sleeves:
With smaller needles, 2 strands of MC, cast on 46 (48, 48) sts and work in k1, p1 rib for 3″ (7.5cm). Inc 8 sts evenly spaced across last row, 54 (56, 56) sts. Change to larger needles and work in st st. Inc 1 st at each end of every 6th row until there are 64 (66, 66) sts. Then inc 1 st each end every 8th row until there are 74 (76, 76) sts. Work evenly until piece measures 19″ (48cm) from beg. Bind off.

Button Band and Collar:
Sew shoulder seams. With smaller needles, 2 strands of MC, cast on 11 sts and work in k1, p1 rib, always sl 1st st and k into back of last st on every row. Work until band measures up front edge to beg of neck shaping, *when slightly stretched*.

Slope Collar:
Row 1: Sl 1, rib to last 2 sts, inc into back of next st, k1 tbl.
Row 2: Sl 1, rib to last st, k1 tbl.
Rep these 2 rows until there are 37 sts on needle. Rib 2 rows, end at straight edge.

Shape Collar:
Next 2 rows: Rib 26 and turn, sl 1, rib to end. Rib 8 rows. Rep these 10 rows once, then rep 2 shaping rows again. Cont in k1, p1 rib until band fits up right front to center back. Bind off in rib. Mark positions for 5 buttons on band, the first ¾″ (2cm) from lower edge and the last at the beg of the collar slope.

Buttonhole Band and Collar:
Work as for buttonband, make buttonholes to correspond with buttons. Buttonhole: sl 1, rib 3, bind off 3, rib 3, k1 tbl. Next row cast on 3 sts over the 3 bound off sts.

Pocket Edging:
With smaller needles, 2 strands of MC, pick up 20 sts from pocket and work in k1, p1 rib for ¾″ (2cm) bind off in rib.

Finishing:
Sew pockets and pocket edging in place. Sew in all ends. Set in sleeves. Sew all seams. Sew on front bands, to button either for a man or woman.

THE HUNTSMAN

Main Color—Red

✕ = Black
○ = Blue
■ = Brown
● = Green
— = Pink
◣ = Rust

Main Color—Grey

✕ = Black
○ = Red
\ = White
■ = Brown
● = Green
— = Pink
◣ = Rust

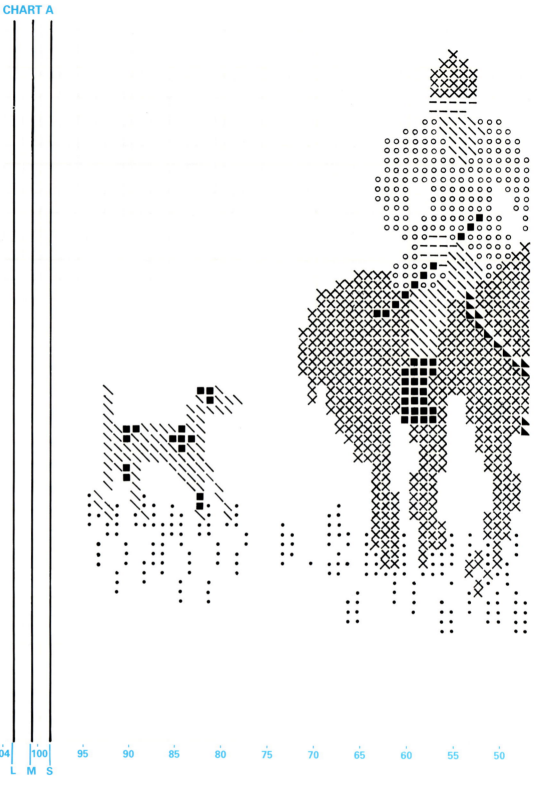

104 100 95 90 85 80 75 70 65 60 55 50
L   M S

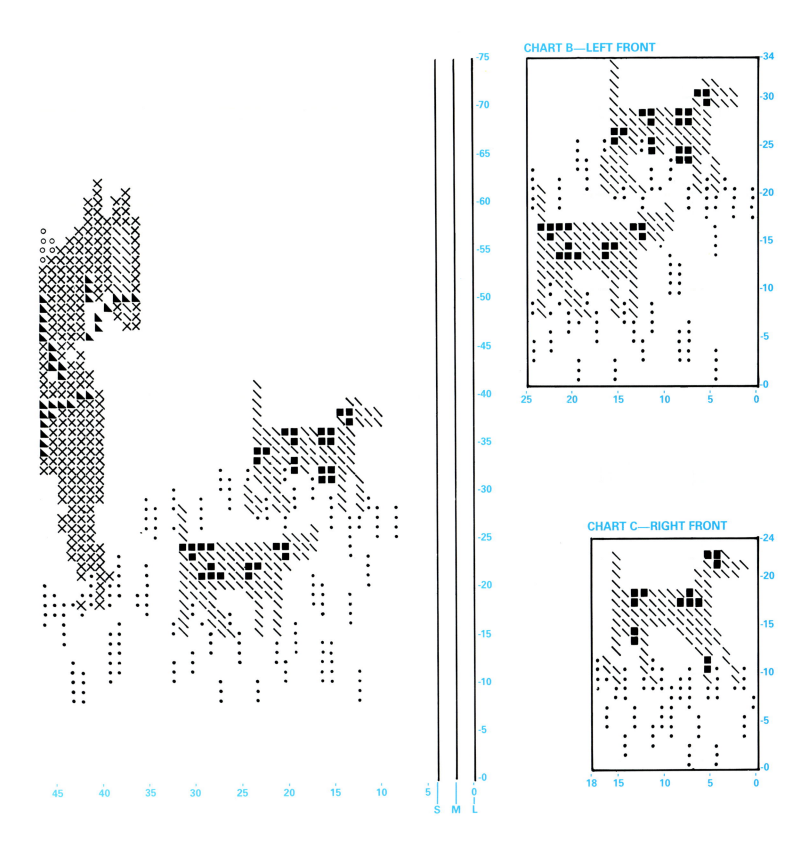

CHART B—LEFT FRONT

CHART C—RIGHT FRONT

VIBRANT CLASSIC

The first of three fabulous Fair Isles. This rich and colorful Fair Isle crew neck, subtly updated, is both relaxed and elegant for daytime warmth and wear. It can be worn endlessly, either casually with jeans or over a soft full skirt and blouse with frilly collar, and will be truly treasured.

Sizes:
To fit 32 (34, 36)″ / 81 (86, 91)cm. Directions are for small with medium and large in parentheses.

Materials:
8 50 gm balls of sportweight wool in MC
1½ 50 gm balls of B
1 50 gm ball for CC's A, C, D, E, F, G, H

Needles:
One pair each #3 (3.25mm), #5 (4mm), #7 (5mm) and #8 (5.5mm), or size needed to obtain gauge.

Gauge:
11 sts = 2″ (5cm) on #7 (5mm) needles over pattern.

Back:
With #3 (3.25mm) needles and MC cast on 88 (94, 100) sts and work in k1, p1 rib for 3″ (7.5cm). Inc 4 sts evenly across row, 92 (98, 104) sts. Change to #7 (5mm) needles and work 4 rows of MC in st st. Begin chart A ("spot" pattern), first knitting 2 sts in MC before repeating pattern across row. Work "spot" pattern until piece measures 12½″ (32cm), or desired length to underarm. (NOTE: End 4 rows after last "spot" row.) Inc 1 st at each end of last row. Change to #8 (5.5mm) needles and begin row 1 of chart B, dec 1 st each side. Cont to work in pattern and dec 1 st each side of every other row. (NOTE: For medium and large sizes, on 64th row dec 1 st each side every row until 66th and 68th row.) On the 64th (66th, 68th) row place the 30 (32, 34) rem sts onto holder for neckband.

Front:
Work as for back until 51st (53rd, 55th) row. Then k2tog, work across pattern for 10 (11, 12) sts then k2tog and turn. Working this side only, cont to dec 1 st at neck and shoulder edge every other row 3 (3, 3) times. Then cont to dec every other row at shoulder edge *at the same time* dec 1 st at neck edge every 4th row 1 (1, 2) times. On last row p2tog. Sl center 18 (20, 22) sts to holder for neck. Join yarn to rem 14 (15, 16) sts and work as for first side, reversing all shaping.

Sleeves:
With #5 (4mm) needles and MC cast on 48 (54, 60) sts and work 4 rows in k1, p1 rib. Begin row 1 of chart C. When 8 rows of chart have been completed repeat chart once more. With MC work 2 rows in st st. Then, 17 rows in k1, p1 rib. (NOTE: The wrong side is now the right side to allow for fold back cuff.) Work 2 rows st st, inc 12 sts across last row, 60 (66, 72) sts. Change to #7 (5mm) needles and work 2 rows of chart D. Then, placing centrally, work 11 rows of chart E. (NOTE: work pattern evenly, *do not* dec as for back.) When 11 rows of chart E are completed, work 2 rows of chart D. Work 4 rows in MC and then begin chart A for "spot" pattern, inc 1 st at each end every other row until there are 84 (90, 96) sts. Cont to work evenly in pattern until piece measures 18″ (46cm), or desired length to underarm from Fair Isle fold back. Inc 4 sts evenly across last row, 88 (94, 100) sts. Change to #8 (5.5mm) needles and begin working row 1 of chart B. Keep pattern correct and dec 1 st at each side every other row until 54th (52nd, 50th) row. Then dec 1 st each side every row until 64th (66th, 68th) row. Sl rem 12 sts to holder for neck.

Neckband:
With #3 (3.25mm) needles and MC and right side facing, beg with left sleeve and pick up 12 sts, 15 (16, 17) sts down left side of front, 18 (20, 22) sts from center front, 15 (16, 17) sts up right front, 12 sts from right sleeve and 30 (32, 34) sts from back. Work in k1, p1 rib for 8 rows. Bind off loosely in rib.

Finishing:
Being sure to match Fair Isle pattern, sew raglan seams. Sew side seams, matching "spot" pattern. Sew sleeve seams. Sew seam neatly on turn back cuff. Weave in all ends.

VIBRANT CLASSIC

A = ×
B = ○
C = /
D = ▽
E = −
F = ●
G = ◢
H = +

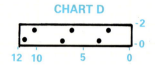

CHART D

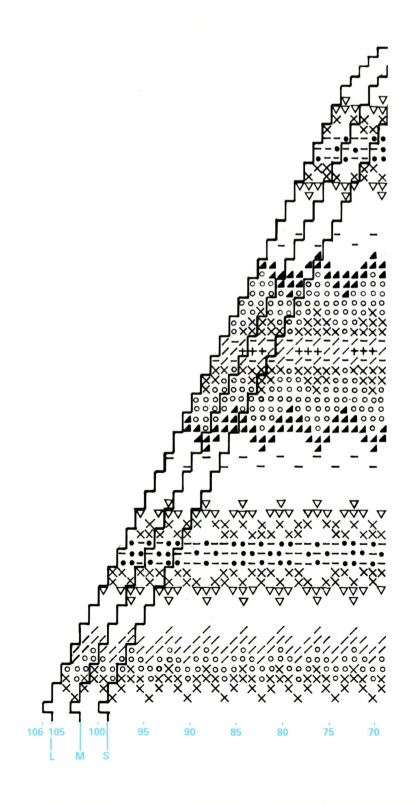

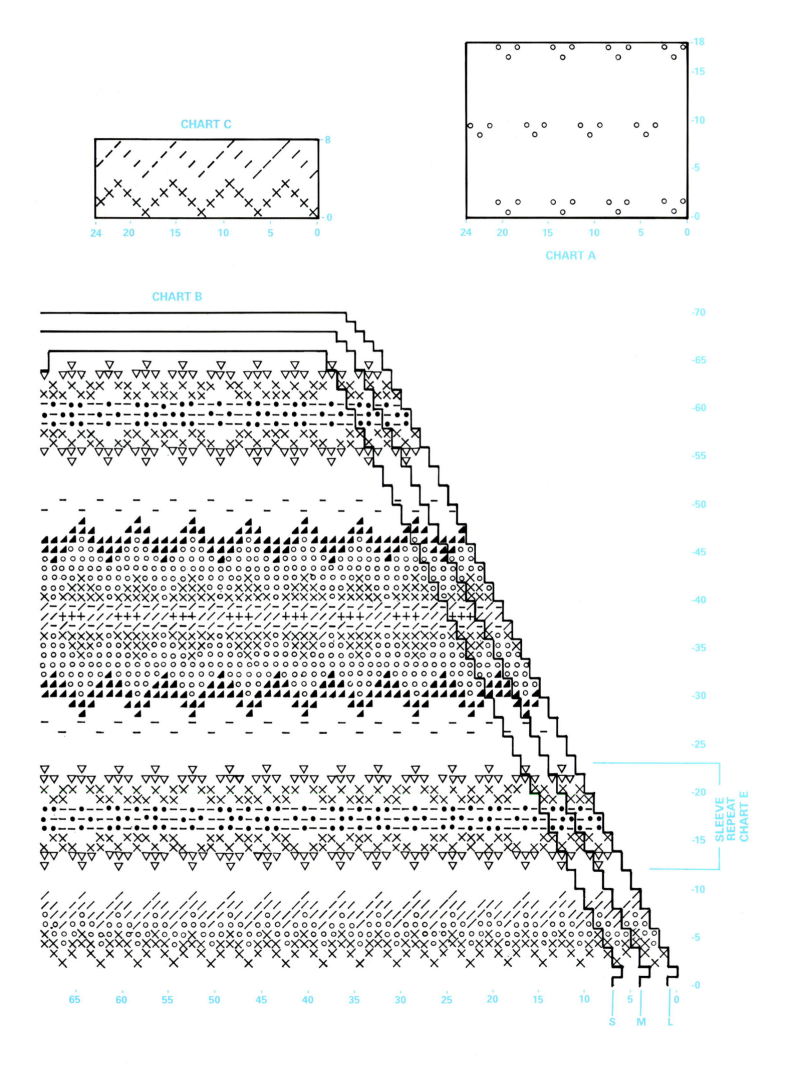

CHART C

CHART A

CHART B

SLEEVE
REPEAT
CHART E

S   M   L

FRONTIER FAIR ISLE

In the same Fair Isle design, this makes a very exciting vest. It's versatile, warm and cozy—and a real pleasure to wear.

Sizes:
To fit small, medium and large. Finished measurements are 38 (40, 42)" / 96 (102, 106)cm. Directions are for small with medium and large in parentheses.

Materials:
9 50 gm balls of bulky wool in MC
2 50 gm balls of B
1 50 gm ball of A, C, F
1 25 gm ball of D, E, G, H
4 buttons

Needles:
One pair each size 5 (4mm) and size 9 (6mm) knitting needles, or size needed to obtain gauge.

Gauge:
15 sts = 4" (10cm) on #9 (6mm) needles over st st.

Back:
With smaller needles and MC cast on 60 (64, 68) sts and work in k1, p1 rib for ¾" (2cm). Change to larger needles and work in st st, *at the same time* inc 1 st at each end of 7th and then every 6th row until there are 68 (72, 76) sts. Work evenly until piece measures 11" (28cm), or desired length to underarm, from beg.

Shape Armholes:
Bind off 3 sts at beg of next 2 rows. Dec 1 st each side of next row, then every other row until 56 (58, 62) sts rem. Work evenly until piece measures 10 (10½, 11)"/ 25 (26.5, 28)cm from armhole bind off. Bind off 10 sts at beg of next 4 rows. Bind off rem 16 (18, 22) sts.

Pockets: (2)
With larger needles and MC cast on 20 sts and work in st st for 5" (13cm). Place these sts on holder.

Left Front:
With smaller needles and MC cast on 41 (43, 45) sts and work in k1, p1 rib with the 3 sts at front edge (last 3 sts) worked in garter st as follows:

Row 1: Sl 1 rib to last 3 sts, k2, k1 tbl.
Row 2: Sl 1 k2, rib to end of row.

When ribbing measures same as back change to larger needles. Keeping 3 end sts in garter border, work 4 rows in st st. Beg chart A ("spot" pattern), repeating pattern across row, except for garter st border which is worked in MC only. When 18 rows of chart have been completed inc 1 st at side edge (beg of row) on next row and then every 6th row until there are 47 (49, 51) sts. *At the same time* when piece measures 5" (13cm) end with right side facing. Work 12 (14, 16) sts, sl next 20 sts onto holder, work 20 sts from pocket lining, work to end. Work evenly in pattern until piece measures 12 rows less than back to armhole. End at front edge. Bind off 3 sts of garter border. Cont to work in pattern until same length as back to armhole. Bind off 3 sts at armhole edge and work row 1 of chart B, k2tog at neck edge. Cont to follow chart B, keeping pattern correct, dec on neck and side edges where indicated on chart. On 50th (52nd, 52nd) row, bind off 10 (11, 12) sts. Work 1 row. Bind off 10 (11, 12) sts. Mark for 4 buttons, the first being 3 rows from bottom, the last on armhole shaping row, and 2 evenly spaced between.

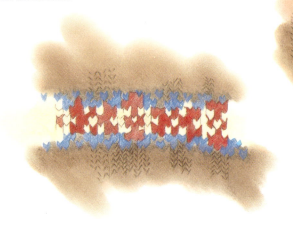

FRONTIER FAIR ISLE

Right Front:
Work as for left front, reversing all shaping *at the same time* making buttonholes. Work 1st buttonhole on 3rd row as follows: Sl 1, k2, k1, p1, k1, yo, k2tog, work to end. Evenly space 3 more buttonholes, the last coming on the armhole shaping row.

Side Shawl Collar: (make 2)
With larger needles and MC cast on 2 sts. Beg row 1 of chart C: k1 row, p1 row. On third row, inc 1 st each side. Cont to follow chart, inc on each side where indicated. On 17th row of chart beg row 1 of Fair Isle pattern. On 64th row bind off in k st.

Back Collar:
With larger needles and MC cast on 39 sts and work 4 rows in st st. Inc 1 st each end of 3rd row. Now work chart A, inc 1 st each end of every 4th row until 45 sts. Work evenly until piece measures 3″ (7.5cm). Then beg 1st row of chart D. When chart is complete repeat these 8 rows once more. Work chart A. Matching first side of collar, dec 1 st each side every 4th row until 39 sts rem. Bind off.

Armbands:
With smaller needles and MC cast on 5 sts and work in k1, p1 rib for 19 (19½, 20)″ / 48 (49.5, 51)cm. Bind off in rib.

Pocket Edgings:
With smaller needles and MC, pick up 20 sts for pocket edging and work 4 rows in k1, p1 rib. Bind off in rib.

Finishing:
Sew side and shoulder seams. Sew on pocket linings and pocket edgings. Turn under garter st border and sew. Being sure to match Fair Isle pattern, join shawl collar to front, across back of neck and other front. Sew in all ends. Fold shawl collar in half and sew into place on inside of vest. Sew on armbands.

FRONTIER FAIR ISLE

A = ×
B = /
C = ▽
D = –
E = ●
F = ◢
G = ○
H = +

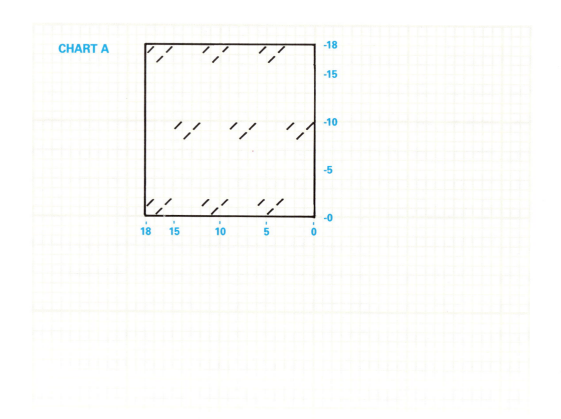

CHART A

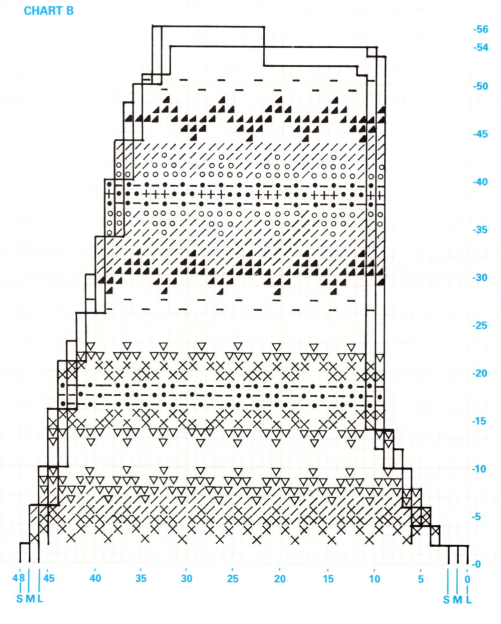

CHART B

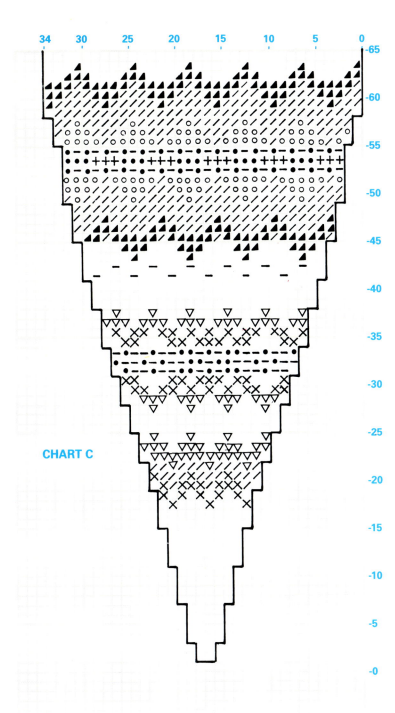

CHART C

CHART D

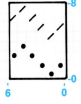

PRAIRIE TREASURE

An old Mexican-style jacket I originally made for my daughter was picked up by Ralph Lauren on one of his many visits to my local center and inspired the creation of this absolutely stunning jacket. He asked me if I could make one in a real Old English Fair Isle design, and this of course was right up my alley. The shape—a cozy wraparound with the gorgeously warm double collar—was hardly changed. Trying pattern after pattern, with masses of beautiful colored wools all round me, I eventually created what I felt he wanted—and I was right. When he returned to London a couple of weeks later the jacket was complete. He put it on and didn't take it off all the time we were working. I still have that original jacket in my wardrobe. I am very

Sizes:
One size large wrap around jacket. This jacket will fit up to 40" (102cm) bust.

Materials:
23 50 gm balls of worsted weight yarn in MC
4 50 gm balls in A
3 50 gm balls in B
2 50 gm balls in C
2 50 gm balls in D
1 50 gm ball in E
2 50 gm balls in F
2 50 gm balls in G
1 25 gm ball in H

Needles:
One pair size 9 (6mm) knitting needles or size needed to obtain gauge.

Gauge:
17 sts and 21 rows = 4" on #9 (6mm) knitting needles over st st.

Back:
With #9 (6mm) knitting needles and MC cast on 90 sts and work in st st for 1½" (4cm). Finish at the end of a purl row. P 2 rows to form ridge hem. Working in st st begin to follow chart for back. Repeat "spot" pattern until piece measures 15" (38 cm) from ridge row. (NOTE: 4 - 6 plain rows should be worked after last "spot" row.) On the last row inc 4 sts evenly across row, 94 sts. Beg row 1 of Fair Isle pattern on back, *at the same time* dec 1 st each end of the 1st row. Cont to dec 1 st each side every other row (as indicated on chart). On 65th row bind off 28 sts.

Pockets: (2)
With #9 (6mm) knitting needles and MC cast on 24 sts and work in st st for 6" (15cm). Place these sts on holder.

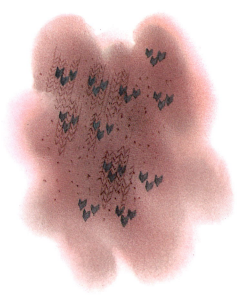

Left front:
With #9 (6mm) knitting needles and MC cast on 60 sts and work in st st for 1½" (4cm). End with a purl row. P 2 rows to form ridge. Beg to work pattern as for back. On row E cast on 10 sts at front edge, work these 10 sts in garter st. Cont to pattern 60 sts and work 10 sts garter until piece is 18 rows less than back to Fair Isle pattern. At the beg of the following row sl 10 garter st band onto holder. Cont to work 60 sts in pattern until piece measures same as back to Fair Isle pattern. Inc 2 sts on last row. Beg row 1 of Fair Isle pattern, *at the same time* dec 1 st each end of 1st row. Cont to dec 1 st each side every other row. On 24th row: beg following left front chart. 25th row: dec 1 st at beg of row. Do not dec at neck edge. Beg dec every 4th row (next front edge dec will be row 27) for neck edge, *at the same time* cont to dec every other row at side edge. Cont dec in this manner until 53rd row. Then finish left front by dec 1 st at each end every other row and cont in Fair Isle pattern as for back, row 54 to 65. Bind off 4 sts.

Right front:
Work as for left front reversing all shaping.

Sleeves:
With #9 (6mm) needles and MC cast on 48 sts and work 4 rows in k1, p1 rib. Then work rows A - H from back chart. (This will be the fold back cuff.) Work 2 rows MC in st st. Then work 15 rows in k1, p1 rib. (NOTE: The wrong side is now facing which will become the right side for the fold back cuff.) K one row. P next row, inc 12 sts evenly spaced across row, 60 sts. Follow chart for sleeve band #2 for 15 rows. On 16th row inc 6 sts evenly spaced across last row. Begin "spot" pattern as for back increasing 1 st at each end every 4th row. When there are 84 sts on needle work evenly until piece measures 18" (46cm) from cast on edge. End with the same number of plain rows as for back. Inc 4 sts evenly spaced across last row, 88 sts. Beg Fair Isle pattern as for back, dec 1 st each

PRAIRIE TREASURE

proud of it—and of the famous and fabulous collection it led to. Wearing it feels really luxurious and deliciously warm. If you wrap it round and snuggle into the beautiful collar, you can face any weather—and it's deceptively easy to knit.

end every other row. (NOTE: The Fair Isle pattern will beg and end the same as back on the odd rows; however for the even rows the pattern will end 6 sts before the end of chart.) On the 54th row dec 1 st at each side. Cont to dec 1 st on each side every row. On 65th row bind off 12 sts.

Side Shawl Collar (make 2):
With #9 (6mm) knitting needles and MC cast on 2 sts. Purl these two sts. Beg to follow chart for shawl collar. Inc in both sts, 4 sts. Next row sl 1, p to last st, k1 tbl. On next row inc into first and last st, 6 sts. Cont to inc 1 st each end every other row. On 8th row begin "spot" pattern. When there are 24 sts begin Fair Isle pattern. Cont to work pattern as established following pattern for back, increasing 1 st each side every other row. On 13th row do not inc. Then work 14th row and inc each side on 15th row. Cont to inc every other row until 23rd row. Inc 1 st each side on this row and then every 3rd row (next inc will be on 26th row). Cont increasing 1 st each side every 3rd row until 59th row. Inc 1 st each side of this row and then every other row twice. On 65th row bind off 74 sts in MC.

Back of Collar:
With #9 (6mm) needles and MC cast on 45 sts and work in "spot" pattern as for back increasing each end of 3rd and every following 4th row until there are 51 sts on needle. Cont in pattern and work evenly until piece measures 3½" (9cm) from beg. End with right side facing. Then using colors F and C (instead of A and F) work rows A - H as for back. Now repeat these 8 rows 3 more times. Work "spot" pattern to match first side, decreasing, instead of increasing, to 45 sts. Bind off in k on wrong side.

Belt:
With #9 (6mm) needles and MC cast on 16 sts and work in k1, p1 rib for 48" (122cm). Bind off in rib.

Front Garter St Edges:
With right side facing and #9 (6mm) needles with MC pick up 10 sts left on holder. Dec 1 st at each end of next and every other row on outside edge until all sts are worked off.

Pocket Edges:
With MC pick up sts left on holder and work 4 rows in k1, p1 rib. Bind off in rib.

Finishing:
Sew off all ends. Sew raglan seams, matching patterns. Sew side edges of back collar to bound off edges of shawl side collar. Pin shawl collar in place matching bound off sts on back collar to back. Match Fair Isle patterns. Cast on point of side collars fits into "V" between jacket front and jacket front edge. With MC, sew into place. Turn front border and shawl collar to inside and sew into place. Sew side seams. Sew pocket linings into place and pocket tops. Turn hem under along hem line and sew into place. Sew sleeve seam to rib, turn sleeve to right side and sew fold back cuff.

Block.

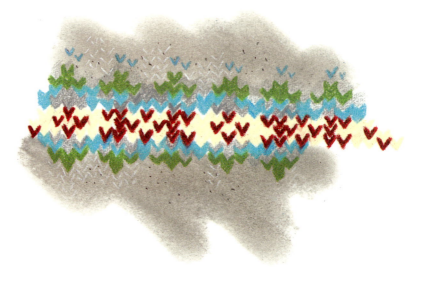

PRAIRIE TREASURE

× = **Turquoise**
◢ = **Rust**
／ = **Brown**
▽ = **Loden Green**
● = **Maroon**
○ = **Jade Green**
− = **Yellow**
＋ = **Pink**

SHAWL COLLAR

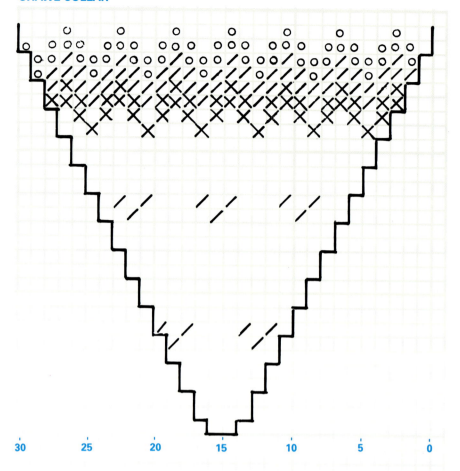

30   25   20   15   10   5   0

SLEEVE BAND #2

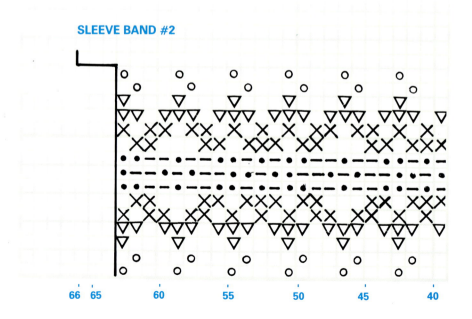

66 65   60   55   50   45   40

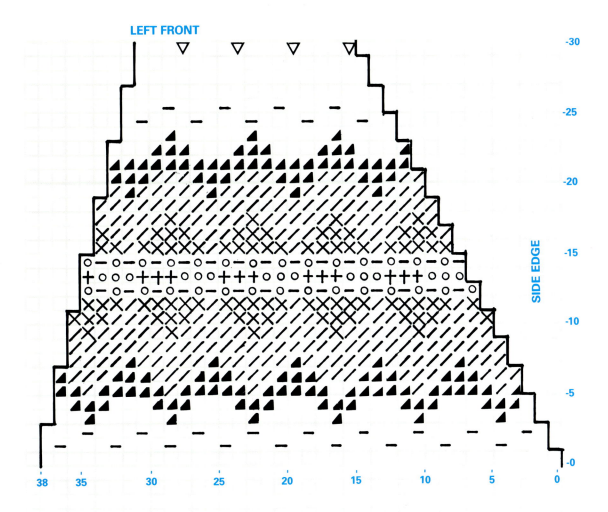

-30

-25

-20

SIDE EDGE

-15

-10

-5

-0

38   35   30   25   20   15   10   5   0

FRONT
EDGE

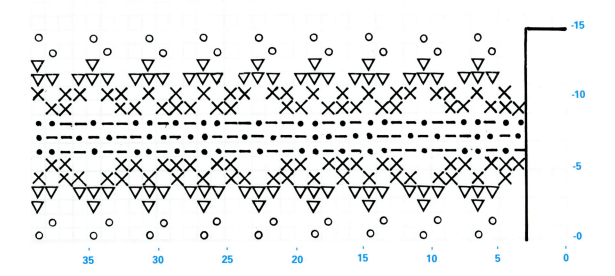

-15

-10

-5

-0

35   30   25   20   15   10   5   0

PRAIRIE
TREASURE

BACK

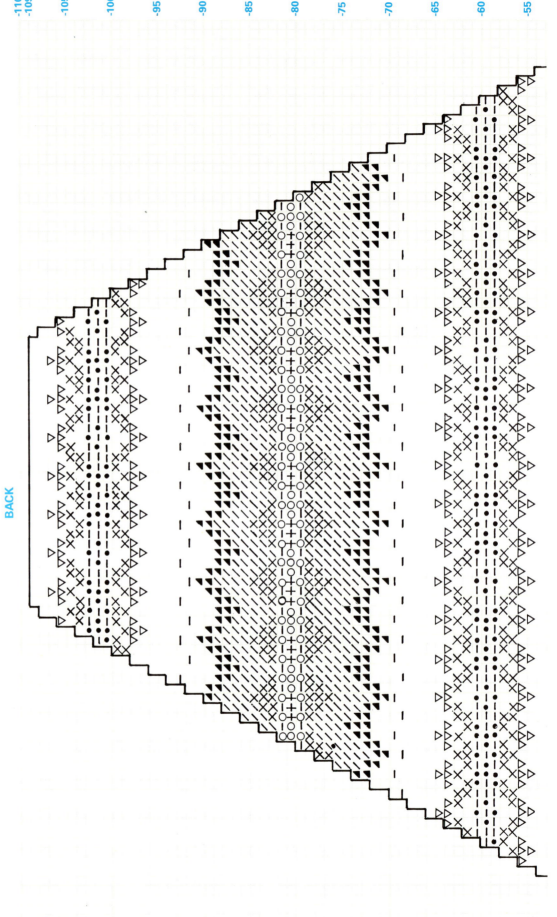

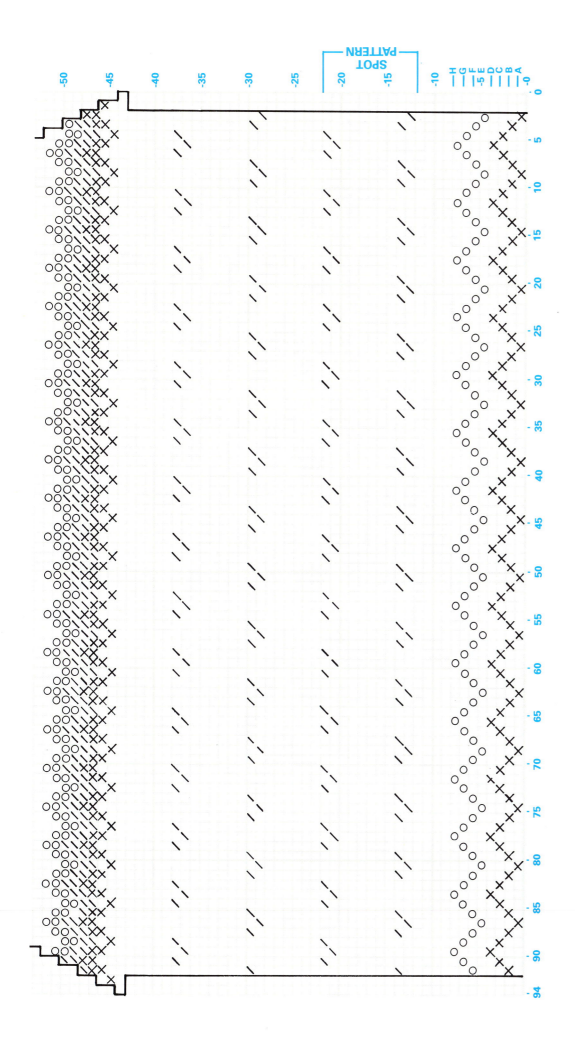

SPOT
PATTERN

A Winter's Yarn

This sweater features subtly changing stitches. With the stand-up collar it is charming on a woman, and without the collar it makes a great men's slash neck sweater. You can make the men's version by binding off at the end of the ridge-stitch yoke and leaving the neck open for about 12" (30 cm).

Sizes:
To fit 38–40" (96–102cm) and 42–44" (106–112cm) chest. This sweater is worn loosely.

Materials:
11 50 gm balls of sportweight yarn

Needles:
One size 3 (3.25mm) and size 5 (4mm) knitting needles for smaller size or size 3 (3.25mm) and size 6 (4.5mm) knitting needles for larger size, or size needed to obtain gauge. One size 2 (3 mm).

Gauge:
22 sts and 28 rows = 4" (10cm) on #6 needles over st st.
For smaller size be sure to check gauge on #6 (4.5mm) needles before decreasing needle size.

Back:
With smaller needles, cast on 100 sts and work in k1, p1 rib for 3" (7.5cm). Inc 20 sts evenly spaced across last row, 120 sts. Change to larger needles and work in st st until piece measures 10" (25cm) from beg. End with right side facing. Then work in pattern as follows:

Row 1: * K9, p1, repeat from * to end.
Row 2: * K2, p7, k1, repeat from * to end.
Row 3: * P2, k5, p2, k1, repeat from * to end.
Row 4: *P2, k2, p3, k2, p1, repeat from * to end.
Row 5: * K2, p2, k1, p2, k3, repeat from * to end.
Row 6: * P4, k3, p3, repeat from * to end.
Row 7: * K4, p1, k5, repeat from * to end.
Row 8: * Purl.

Work 6 rows in st st.
These 14 rows form pattern 1. Repeat these 14 rows twice more, then work the first 8 rows once.

Shape Armholes:
Bind off 10 sts at beg of next 2 rows. Work evenly in st st until piece measures 20" (50.5cm) from beg. End with right side facing. Work diamond pattern as follows:

Row 1: *K8, p1, k11, repeat from * to end.
Row 2: *P10, k3, p7, repeat from * to end.
Row 3: *K6, p5, k9, repeat from * to end.
Row 4: *P8, k7, p5, repeat from * to end.
Row 5: *K4, p9, k7, repeat from * to end.

Row 6: *P6, k11, p3, repeat from * to end.
Row 7: *K2, p13, k5, repeat from * to end.
Row 8: Work as for row 6.
Row 9: Work as for row 5.
Row 10: Work as for row 4.
Row 11: Work as for row 3.
Row 12: Work as for row 2.
Row 13: Work as for row 1.
Row 14: Purl.

Work 4 rows in st st. End with right side facing. Work in ridge st as follows:

Row 1: Purl.
Row 2: Knit.
Row 3: Knit.
Row 4: Purl.

Repeat these 4 rows until work measures 27" (68.5cm) from beg. End with right side facing.

Shape Shoulders:
Bind off 28 sts at beg of next 2 rows, 44 sts. Change to #2 (3mm) needles and work in k1, p1 rib for ¾" (2cm). Change to #3 (3.25mm) needles and work in seed st for 3" (7.5cm). Bind off loosely in rib.

Front:
Work as for back until shoulder shaping. Then, bind off 28 sts at beg of next 2 rows, 44 sts. Change to #2 (3mm) needles and work in k1, p1 rib for ¾" (2cm). Change to #3 (3.25mm) needles and work in seed st across 22 sts and turn. Work in seed st for 3" (7.5mm) Bind off loosely in rib. Join yarn to rem 22 sts and work to match first side.

Sleeves:
With #3 (3.25mm) needles, cast on 48 sts and work in k1, p1 rib for 3" (7.5cm). Inc into every other st across last row, 72 sts. Change to larger needles and work in st st, *at the same time* inc 1 st at each end of the 5th row, then every 4th row until there are 90 sts. Work evenly until piece measures 10" (26cm), Work pattern 1 (zigzag) as on back. Work evenly until piece measures 19½" (49.5). Bind off.

Finishing:
Sew shoulder and collar seams (collar opens at front). Sew in sleeves by placing top of side edges of sleeves to bound off sts of armhole. Sew side and sleeve seams.

Collectible Cottons

The cotton handknit market has changed dramatically in recent years. Cotton handknits have become much more popular, and to meet this new demand yarn manufacturers are producing exciting and varied selections of cotton. ■ Cotton accentuates bold textured designs and gives richer clarity of color. The finished garments can look really dramatic. For this reason I mainly use a matt (non-mercerised) sportweight cotton for my novelty textured or motif/Fair Isle sweaters. For delicate lacy or textured designs, I use a fine mercerised cotton which gives a silky, very expensive look. ■ A cotton garment will always weigh more than its equivalent in wool (e.g. A Summer Sculpture in this section takes 5 x 50 gm balls more in cotton than in wool). Because of their extra weight and lack of elasticity, cottons do not keep their shape as well as wool—ribs, particularly, are inclined to stretch. To minimize this, the garments are knitted on smaller needles to give a firm tension. ■ These sweaters should also be washed and dried carefully. Cotton does wash very well in a washing machine but be sure colors are fast when you buy the yarn. Machine wash on a gentle cycle (preferably in a mesh bag) and then spin dry. Hand smooth and fold garments into shape before drying even if you are using a tumble dryer (which should, incidentally, be on a low setting). Cotton responds well to pressing, but, of course, do not press heavily textured sweaters. ■ The freshness and beauty of a cotton garment is well worth the extra effort of maintenance.

A SUMMER SCULPTURE

This sweater really is extraordinarily beautiful. Making it will give you a wonderful feeling of satisfaction and achievement. It is not very difficult to knit—the front is slow with all its bobbles, but that's all and it is well worth the effort. Photographed here in white, it is also lovely in pastel or bright colors. For cooler weather it can just as easily be made in sportweight wool.

Sizes:

One size. This is a loose oversized sweater that has a finished measurement of 42" (106cm). To make a larger size, go up one needle size. (NOTE: Be sure to check gauge as required for pattern before advancing needle size.)

Materials:

20 50 gm balls of sportweight cotton

Needles:

One pair each size 2 (3mm) and size 5 (4mm) or size needed to obtain gauge.

Gauge:

13 sts = 2" (5cm) on #5 (4mm) needles over st st.

Abbreviations:

kB = knit into back of stitch.
pB = purl into back of stitch.
TWL = Twist left-k into back of 2nd st, then k 1st st and sl both sts off needle tog.
TWR = Twist right-lift up 2nd st and k into it, k 1st st and sl both sts off needle tog.
Seed stitch = k1, p1 all along row. (If row ends k1, the next row will begin k1, or vice versa).
yo = yarn over.
wyfnt = with yarn in front.
psso = pass slipped stitch over.
sl = slip.
yf = yarn front.
ssk = sl 1st and 2nd sts knitwise one at a time, then insert the tip of left hand needle into the fronts of these 2 sts from the left, and k them tog from this position.
P2 SS0 = Pass 2 sl sts over.

LONG CABLE = LC.
Rows 1, 3, 5: k 8.
Rows 2, 4, 6: p 8.
Row 7: C4B by slipping next 4 sts onto cable needle and leave at back of work, k4 then k4 from cable needle.
Row 8: p 8.
Rows 9, 11: k 8.
Rows 10, 12: p 8.

DOUBLE CABLE = DC.
Row 1: k 12.
Row 2: p 12.
Row 3: C6B by slipping next 3 sts onto cable needle and leave at back of work, k3, then k3 from cable needle, C6F by slipping next 3 sts onto cable needle and leave at front of work, k3, then k3 from cable needle.

Rows 4, 6, 8: p 12.
Rows 5, 7: k 12.

TREE OF LIFE AND RIB PATTERN

Row 1: Single rib 8, * p3, k3B, p3, rib 8, rep from * to end.
Row 2: Single rib 8, * k3, p3B, k3, rib 8, rep from * to end.
Row 3: Single rib 8, * p2, TWR, k1B, TWL, p2, rib 8, rep from * to end.
Row 4: Single rib 8, * k2, (p1B, k1) twice, p1B, k2, rib 8, rep from * to end.
Row 5: Single rib 8, * p1, TWR, p1, k1B, p1, TWL, p1, rib 8, rep from * to end.
Row 6: Single rib 8, * k1, p1B, k2, p1B, k2, p1B, k1, rib 8, rep from * to end.
Row 7: Single rib 8, * TWR, p1, k3B, p1, TWL, rib 8, rep from * to end.
Row 8: Single rib 8, * p1B, k2, p3B, k2, p1B, rib 8, rep from * to end.
Row 9: Single rib 8, * p2, TWR, k1B, TWL, p2, rib 8, rep from * to end.
Rep rows 4-9 inclusive.

Back:

With smaller needles, cast on 110 sts and work in "Tree of Life and Rib Pattern" for 3" (7.5cm). Inc 30 sts evenly spaced across last row, 140 sts. Change to larger needles and set pattern as follows:

Row 1: Sl 1, seed 8, p2, DC (row 1), p3, LC (row 1), p1, TWR, p1, seed 64, p1, TWL, p1, LC (row 1), p3, DC (row 1), p2, seed 8, k1, tbl.

A SUMMER SCULPTURE

Row 2: Sl 1, seed 8, k2, DC (row 2), k3, LC (row 2), k1, p2, k1, seed 64, k1, p2, k1, LC (row 2), k3, DC (row 2), k2, seed 8, k1 tbl.

With pattern set, work DC and LC cables on correct rows, (after 24 rows both DC and LC will be back to row 1). Cont in pattern and work evenly until back measures 26″ (66cm) from beg. End with right side facing.

Shape Shoulders:

Keeping pattern correct, bind off 15 sts at beg of next 6 rows (NOTE: when binding off across DC and LC cables, work center 2 sts tog.) Place rem 50 sts on holder for neckband.

Front:

Work as for back until "Tree of Life and Rib Pattern" has been completed. Change to larger needles and pattern as follows:

Row 1: Sl 1, seed 8, p2, DC (row 1), p3, LC (row 1), p1, TWR, p1, p64, p1, TWL, p1, LC (row 1), p3, DC (row 1), p2, seed 8, k1 tbl.
Row 2: Sl 1, seed 8, k2, DC (row 2), k3, LC (row 2), k1, p2, k1, k64, k1, p2, k1, LC (row 2), k3, DC (row 2), k2, seed 8, k1 tbl.

With pattern set, cont until front measures 6″ (15cm) from beg. End with right side facing. With pattern set each side of center 64 sts, work center 64 sts in sculptured front, following chart. (NOTE: Be careful to keep DC and LC cables correct.) After last row of chart, cont in reverse st st until work measures 23½″ (60cm) from cast on edge, ending with right side facing.

Shape Neck:

Pattern 55 sts and turn. Working this side only, dec 1 st at neck edge every row until 45 sts rem. Cont in pattern until piece measures 26″ (66cm) from beg. End with right side facing.

Shape Shoulder:

Bind off 15 sts at beg of next row and then every other row twice (NOTE: work center 2 sts tog on DC and LC cable). Return to rem sts and sl 30 center sts onto holder for neckband. Join yarn and work to match first side.

Sleeves:

With smaller needles, cast on 42 sts and work "Tree of Life and Rib Pattern" for 3″ (7.5cm). Inc 22 sts evenly spaced across last row, 64 sts. Change to larger needles and set pattern as follows:
Sl 1, seed 6, p2, TWL, p2, DC, p3, LC, p3, DC, p2, TWR, p2, seed 6, k1 tbl. Cont to work in pattern and inc 1 st each end of next row and then every 4th row until there are 126 sts, work increased sts into seed st. Work evenly until piece measures 19″ (48cm) from beg. End with right side facing. Working 2 sts tog over cables, bind off.

Neckband:

Sew right shoulder seam. With smaller needles and right side facing, pick up 23 sts down left side of neck, 30 sts from center front, 23 sts up right side of neck and 50 sts from back, 126 sts. Work in "Tree of Life and Rib Pattern" (working 6 sts in rib instead of 8) for 1¼″ (3cm). Bind off in pattern.

Finishing:

Sew left shoulder seam. Sew in sleeves, placing center of sleeve to shoulder seam. Sew side and sleeve seams.

A Summer Sculpture

KEY:

- • = rev st st
- □ = blank = st st
- ● = k on right side in the back of st p on wrong side in the back of st
- ✓╱ = BC = sl 1 st onto cable needle and leave at back of work, k1, then p1 from cable needle
- ╲ = FC = sl 1 st onto cable needle and leave at front of work, p1, then k1 from cable needle
- ╱╱ = TWR = Twist Right = lift 2nd st and k into it, k 1st st and sl both sts off needle tog
- ╲╲ = TWL = Twist Left = k into back of 2nd st, then k 1st st and sl both sts off needle tog
- ╱╴ = BPC = same as BC but p both sts
- ╱ = BKC = same as BC but k both sts
- ╲ = FKC = same as FC but k both sts
- ╲╴ = FPC = same as FC but p both sts
- ⁵ = p1, yo, p1, yo, p1 into next st
- ₅ = sl 2, wyfnt, p3 tog, p2 sso
- ⁴ = k1, p1, k1, p1 into next st
- ⁴ = sl 3, k1, pass 3rd, 2nd, 1st over k st
- ³ = k1, yo, k1
- ₃ = p3 tog
- ◇ = bobble large = k1, p1, k1, p1 into st, turn, k4, turn, p4, sl 2nd, 3rd, and 4th sts over 1st
- ↓ = purl into front and back and front again of next st
- 2 = k 3 sts
- 3 = purl into front and back of next st, p1, purl into front and back of next st
- 5 = purl into front and back of next st, p3, purl into front and back of next st
- 4 = k 5 sts
- 6 = k 7 sts
- 7 = p2 tog, p3, p2 tog.
- 8 = k 5 sts
- 9 = p2 tog, p1, p2 tog.
- 10 = k3
- AA = k2 tog., then k same 2 sts tog again through front loops
- A/A = p1, yo, p1
- A\A = ssk, k1
- ∨ = k into front and back of next st
- ∧ = p2 tog
- ⟍ = sl 2, k1, p2 sso

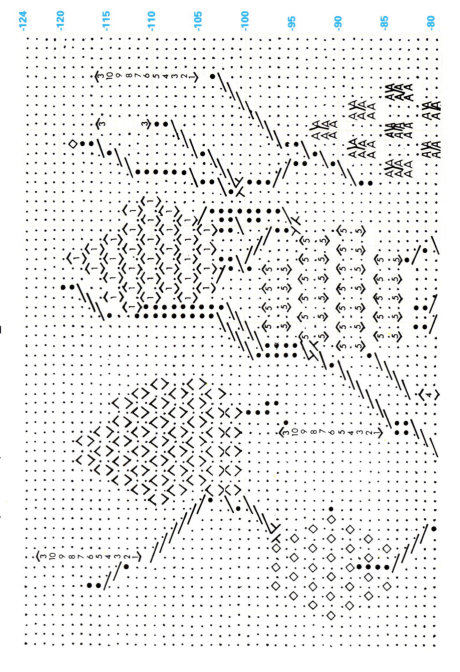

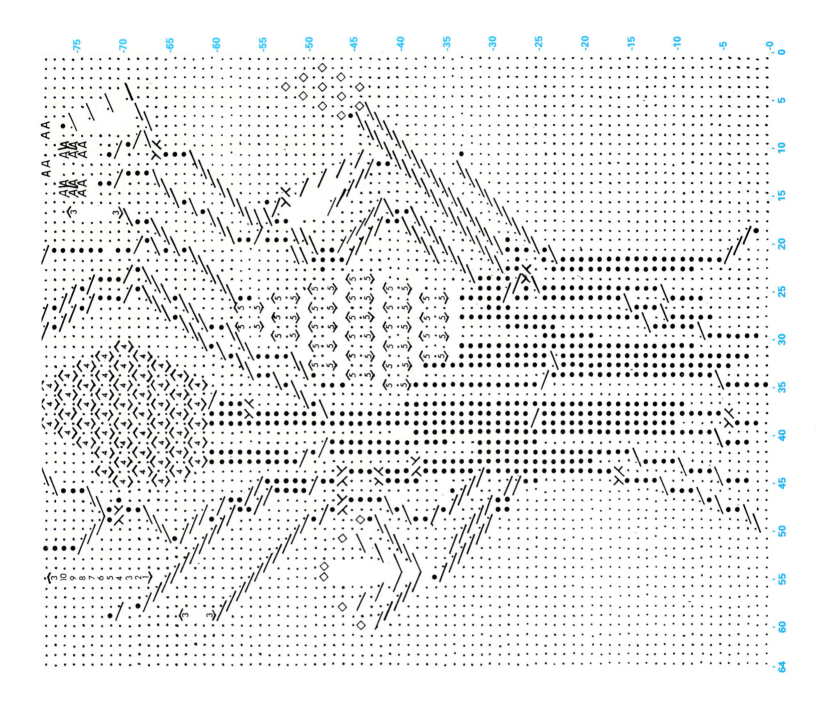

ULTRA MARINE

Nautical designs seem to be here to stay. I find they are ordered from me year after year. When I was first asked to "think nautical," I got books out of the Maritime Museum in Greenwich here in England, to give me ideas and outlines. This sweater is one of the results.

Sizes:
To fit 34 (36, 38, 40)″ / 86 (91, 96, 102)cm bust. Directions are for small with the larger sizes in parentheses.

Materials:
11 50 gm balls sportweight cotton in MC Small amounts of sportweight cotton in 10 CC

Needles:
One pair each size 2 (3mm) and size 5 (4mm) knitting needles or size needed to obtain gauge.

Gauge:
11 sts = 2″ (5cm) on #5 (4mm) needles over st st.

Back:
With smaller needles, cast on 86 (90, 94, 98) sts and work in k1, p1 rib for 3″ (7.5cm). Inc 10 sts evenly spaced across last row 96 (100, 104, 108) sts. Change to larger needles and work 6 rows in st st. Then set chart A as follows: Sl 1, k6, work across 44 sts of row 1 of chart, k to end. With pattern set cont to work in chart until complete. Then work in MC until back measures 15″ (38cm) from beg. End with right side facing.

Shape Armholes:
Bind off 4 sts at beg of next 4 rows. Work evenly until piece measures 23 (23, 24, 24)″ / 58.5 (58.5, 61, 61)cm from beg. End with right side facing.

Shape Shoulders:
Bind off 10 (11, 12, 13)sts at beg of next 4 rows. Leave rem 40 sts on holder for neckband.

Front:
Work rib as for back. Change to larger needles and work from chart B which is set as follows: K3 (5, 7, 9) sts, work across 90 sts of chart, k to end. Work up chart until front measures same as back to armhole. Shape armholes as for back. Cont to follow chart until front measures 20½ (20½, 21½, 21½)″ / 52 (52, 54.5, 54.5)cm from beg. End with right side facing. (NOTE: When chart is complete work in MC.)

Shape Neck:
Work across 25 (27, 29, 31) sts, turn and work back. Working this side only, dec 1 st at neck edge on next and then every other row until 20 (22, 24, 26) sts rem. Work evenly until front measures same as back to shoulder. End with right side facing.

Shape Shoulder:
Bind off 10 (11, 12, 13) sts at beg of next row. Work 1 row, then rep bind off. Sl 30 center sts onto a holder for neckband. Join yarn and work as for first side, reversing all shaping.

Sleeves:
With smaller needles, cast on 76 sts and work in k1, p1 rib for 1″ (2.5cm). Inc 4 sts evenly across last row, 80 sts. Change to larger needles and work in st st until sleeve measures 4½″ (11cm) from beg. End with right side facing.

Shape cap:
Bind off 5 sts at beg of next 2 rows. Then dec 1 st at each end of next 19 rows. Bind off in k on next wrong side row.

Neckband:
Sew right shoulder seam. With right side facing and smaller needles, pick up 14 sts down left side of neck, 30 sts from center front, 14 sts up right side of neck and 40 sts from back. Work 4 rows in k1, p1 rib. Bind off in rib.

Finishing:
Sew left shoulder seam. Sew sleeves into armholes. Sew side and sleeves seams. Sew in all ends.

ULTRA MARINE

Base = Navy
- ● = Pale Blue
- ● = White
- ✕ = Beige
- ◤ = Red
- ▼ = Yellow
- △ = Turquoise
- / = Brown
- ○ = Pink

CHART A—BACK—BOAT MOTIF

CHART B—FRONT

-75
-70
-65
-60
-55
-50
-45
-40
-35
-30
-25
-20
-15
-10
-5
-0
90
85
80
75
70
65
60
55
50
45
40
35
30
25
20
15
10
5
0

PALMS AND SAILS

Hers

Another top favorite among my cotton sweaters and an enormous favorite with men. The dramatic coconut palm and colorful boat make it really exciting and there are six different color bases.

Sizes:
To fit 34 (36, 38, 40)" / 86 (91, 97, 102)cm chest. Directions are for the small size with the larger sizes in parentheses.

Materials:
9 (10, 10, 11) 50 gm balls of sportweight cotton in MC
1 50 gm ball in CC
small quantities of other colors

Needles:
One pair each size 2 (3mm) and size 5 (4mm) knitting needles or size needed to obtain gauge.

Gauge:
11 sts = 2" (5cm) on #5 needles worked in st st.

Back:
With smaller needles and MC, cast on 86 (90, 94, 98) sts and work in k1, p1 rib for 3" (7.5 cm). Inc 10 sts evenly spaced across last row, 96 (100, 104, 108) sts. Change to larger needles and work 6 rows in st st. Row 7: Sl 1, k6, k27 sts of row 1 of chart A, k to end. Cont until chart A is completed, then cont in st st until back measures 15" (38 cm) from beg. End with right side facing.

Shape Armholes:
Bind off 4 sts at beg of next 4 rows, then work evenly until piece measures 23 (23, 24, 24)" / 58.5 (58.5, 61, 61)cm from beg. End with right side facing.

Shape Shoulders:
Bind off 10 (11, 12, 13) sts at beg of next 4 rows. Place rem 40 sts on holder for neckband.

Front:
Work ribbing as for back. Change to larger needles and work from chart B as follows: k3 (5, 7, 9) work across 90 sts of chart, k to end. Follow chart until front measures same as back to armholes. End with right side facing.

Shape Armholes:
Work as for back. Cont to follow chart B until front measures 20 ½ (20 ½, 21, 21)" / 52 (52, 53, 53)cm from beg. End with right side facing. (NOTE: When chart is complete work in MC.)

Shape Neck:
K across 25 (27, 29, 31) sts, turn and p back. Dec 1 st at neck edge on next row, then every other row 4 times, 20 (22, 24, 26) sts. Work evenly until piece measures same as back to shoulder. End with right side facing.

Shape Shoulder:
Bind off 10 (11, 12, 13) sts at beg of next row and then every other row once. Place 30 center sts on holder for neck. Join yarn and work left side to correspond to right, reversing all shaping.

Short Sleeves:
With smaller needles and MC, cast on 76 sts and work in k1, p1 rib for 1" (2.5cm). Inc 4 sts evenly across last row, 80 sts. Change to larger needles and work in st st until sleeve measures 4½" (11cm) from beg. End with right side facing.

Shape Cap:
Bind off 5 sts at beg of next 2 rows, then dec 1 st at each end of every row 19 times. Bind off with wrong side facing.

Neckband:
Sew right shoulder seam. With smaller needles and MC, pick up 14 sts down left side of neck, 30 sts from center front, 14 sts up right side of neck and 40 sts from back, 98 sts. Work in k1, p1 rib for 3 rows. Bind off loosely in rib.

Finishing:
Sew left shoulder seam. Sew in all ends. Sew in sleeves and side seams.

PALMS AND SAILS

His

Sizes:
May be a loose sweater for women, fitted for men. To fit 40 (42, 44, 46)" / 102 (106, 112, 117)cm chest. Directions are for small with larger sizes in parentheses.

Materials:
16 (16, 17, 17) 50 gm sportweight cotton in MC
1 50 gm ball in main CC, small amounts of all other colors (see chart)

Needles:
One pair each size 2 (3mm) and size 5 (4mm) knitting needles or size needed to obtain gauge.

Gauge:
13 sts = 2½" (6cm) on #5 needles worked in st st.

Back:
With smaller needles and MC, cast on 98 (102, 106, 110) sts and work in k1, p1 rib for 3" (7.5cm). Inc 10 sts evenly across last row, 108 (112, 116, 120) sts. Change to larger needles and work in st st for 2½ (2½, 3)" / 6 (6, 7.5, 7.5)cm. End with right side facing. Work chart A as follows: Sl 1, k6, k27 sts of row 1 of chart A, k to end. Cont until chart A is completed, then cont in st st until back measures 18" (46cm) from beg. End with right side facing.

Shape Armholes:
Bind off 4 sts at beg of next 2 rows. Work evenly until piece measures 26½ (27, 27½, 28)" / 67 (68.5, 70, 71)cm from beg. End with right side facing.

Shape Shoulders:
Bind off 14 (15, 16, 17) sts at beg of next 4 rows. Place rem 44 sts on holder for neckband.

Front:
Work ribbing as for back. Change to larger needles and work in st st for 2½ (2½, 3, 3)" / 6 (6, 7.5, 7.5)cm. End with right side. Work from chart B as follows: K9 (11, 13, 15) st, k across 90 sts of chart, k to end. Follow chart until front measures same as back to armholes. End with right side facing.

Shape Armholes:
Work as for back. Cont to follow chart B until front measures 23½ (24, 24½, 25)" / 60 (61, 62, 63.5)cm from beg. End with right side facing. (NOTE: When chart is complete work in MC.)

Shape Neck:
K across 33 (35, 37, 39) sts, turn and p back. Dec 1 st at neck edge on next row, then every other row 4 times, 28 (30, 32, 34) st. Work evenly until front measures same as back to shoulder. End with right side facing.

Shape Shoulders:
Bind off 14 (15, 16, 17) sts at beg of next row and then every other row once. Place center 34 sts onto holder for neck edge. Join yarn and work left side to correspond to right, reversing all shaping.

Right Sleeve:
With smaller needles and MC, cast on 44 sts and work in k1, p1 rib for 3" (7.5cm). Inc 10 sts evenly across last row, 54 sts. Change to larger needles and work in st st, *at the same time* inc 1 st each side of 7th row and then every 6th row until there are 80 (82, 82, 84) sts. Work evenly until piece measures 19 (19, 19½, 20)" / 48 (48, 49.5, 51)cm from beg. End with right side facing.

Shape Cap:
Bind off 5 sts at beg of next 2 rows, then dec 1 st each side every row 19 times. Bind off with wrong side facing.

Left Sleeve:
Work as for right sleeve, but work in chart C when sleeve measures 8" (20cm) from beg. Set chart C as follows: Sl 1, k26, k across 32 sts of chart C, k to end. Cont to work up chart until complete, then work as for right sleeve.

Neckband:
Sew right shoulder seam. With smaller needles and MC, pick up 14 sts down left side of neck, 34 sts from center front, 14 sts up right side of neck and 44 sts from back, 106 sts. Work in k1, p1 rib for 3 rows. Bind off loosely in rib.

Finishing:
Sew left shoulder seam. Sew in ends. Sew in sleeves and sew side and sleeve seams.

PALMS AND SAILS

Base = Yellow
/ = Rust
× = Mid Brown
◤ = Bright Green
◇ = White
— = Beige
▲ = Dark Brown
■ = Bottled Green
● = Red
• = Navy
• = Orange
▼ = Royal Blue

CHART A—BACK MOTIF

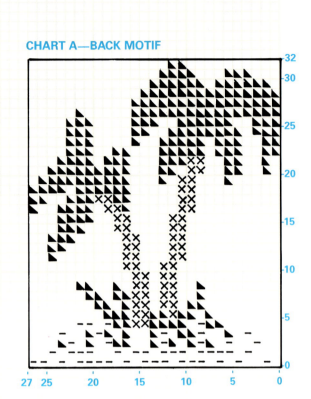

CHART C—LEFT SLEEVE

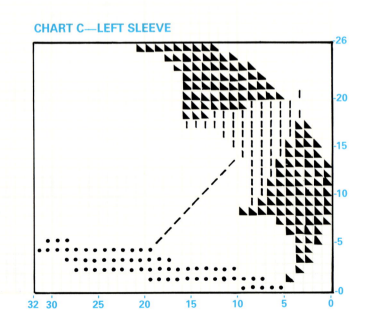

BRIGHT LINES

Continuing the bright and cheerful summer look, this Fair Isle vest is a very useful garment. It's so simple to knit, and you can do it in an endless number of different colors. Charming when worn with trousers or skirts, with or without a shirt, it's a highly practical garment.

REPEAT ACROSS ROW

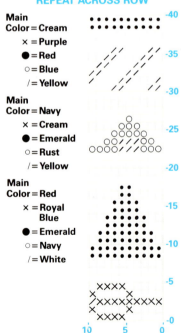

Main Color = Cream
× = Purple
● = Red
○ = Blue
/ = Yellow

Main Color = Navy
× = Cream
● = Emerald
○ = Rust
/ = Yellow

Main Color = Red
× = Royal Blue
● = Emerald
○ = Navy
/ = White

Sizes:
To fit small, medium, large. Finished bust measurements 36 (40, 44)″ / 91 (102, 112)cm. Directions are for small with medium and large in parentheses.

Materials:
7 (8, 9) 50 gm balls sportweight cotton in cream
2 50 gm balls sportweight cotton in red
1 50 gm ball sportweight cotton in purple, blue, yellow

Needles:
One pair each size 2 (3mm) and size 5 (4mm) knitting needles, or size needed to obtain gauge.

Gauge:
11 sts = 2″ (5cm) on #5 (4mm) needles over st st.

Back:
With smaller needles and MC, cast on 90 (100, 110) sts and work in k1, p1 rib for 8 rows. Inc 10 sts evenly across last row, 100 (110, 120) sts. Change to larger needles and work pattern following chart. (The pattern is repeated 10 (11, 12) times across row.) Repeat rows 1 through 40 until piece measures 17″ (43cm) from beg. End with right side facing.

Shape Armholes:
Cont to work in pattern and bind off 4 sts at beg of next 2 rows. Then dec 1 st at each side every other row 6 times, 80 (90, 100) sts. Cont in pattern until piece measures 27″ (68.5 cm) from beg. End with right side facing.

Shape Shoulders:
Cont to work in pattern and bind off 10 (12, 14) sts at beg of next 4 rows. Place rem 40 (42, 44) sts on holder for neckband.

Pocket Linings:
With larger knitting needles and MC, cast on 26 (30, 34) sts and work in st st for 5½″ (14cm). Place these sts on holder. (Make two pocket linings.)

Front:
Work as for back until front measures 6½″ (16.5 cm) from beg. End with right side facing. Cont to work in pattern, pattern 10 sts, sl next 26 (30, 34) sts onto holder,

pattern across 26 (30, 34) sts of first pocket, pattern 28 (30, 32) sts, sl next 26 (30, 34) sts onto holder, pattern across 26 (30, 34) sts of second pocket, pattern 10. Cont in pattern until front measures same as back to armhole, ending with right side facing.

Shape Armholes:
Cont to work in pattern and bind off 4 sts at beg of next 2 rows. Then dec 1 st at each side every other row 6 times, 80 (90, 100) sts.

Shape Neck:
Pattern across 40 (45, 50) sts and turn. Then dec 1 st at neck edge on next and then every third row until 20 (24, 28) sts rem. Work in pattern until piece measures same as back to shoulder. End with right side facing.

Shape Shoulder:
Bind off 10 (12, 14) sts at beg of next row. Work 1 row. Bind off 10 (12, 14) sts at beg of next row. Join yarn to rem sts and work as for first side, reversing all shaping.

Neckband:
Sew in ends. Join right shoulder seam. Beg at left shoulder with smaller needles and right side facing, with MC pick up and knit 50 sts down left side of front neck, pick up and mark center st, 50 sts up right side, and 40 (42, 44) sts from back, 141 (143, 145) sts. Work in k1, p1 rib for 6 rows, knitting 3 center front sts tog on every row, including bind off. Bind off in rib.

Armbands:
Sew left shoulder seam. With smaller needles and MC beg at underarm and pick up 60 sts each side of shoulder seam, 120 sts in all. Work 6 rows in k1, p1 rib, k2tog at beg and end of every row. Bind off in rib.

Pocket Edging:
With smaller needles and MC pick up 26 (30, 34) sts from pocket. Work 4 rows in k1, p1 rib. Bind off in rib.

Finishing:
Sew pocket linings and edging into place. Sew side seams.

TYROL TREASURE

I have a very special soft spot for this lovely little cardigan. Originally I designed it for a young and lively boutique in Stockholm, and since then I've done it in both cotton and wool. It has become one of my real classics.

You will notice in the written pattern that there is a cord at the neck as well as a ripple bind off, whereas in the photograph the neck is plain garter stitch, and bound off plain. So many have been made either way that it's really a personal choice. It's also beautiful with or without the embroidery. I love it—it's such a soft "feminine" cardigan.

Sizes:
To fit 32 (34, 36, 38)″ / 81 (86, 91, 96)cm bust. Directions are for small with larger sizes in parentheses.

Materials:
8 (8, 9, 9) 50 gm balls of sportweight yarn

Needles:
One pair each size 3 (3.25mm) and size 8 (5.5mm), or size needed to obtain gauge.

Gauge:
11 sts = 2″ (5cm) on #8 needles over pattern.

Abbreviations:
MB = Make Bobble = (k1, p1, k1) into next st, turn, k3, turn, p3, then sl 2nd and 3rd over first st.

Back:
With smaller needles, cast on 88 (92, 96, 104) sts and work in k1, p1 rib for 4″ (10cm). On last rib row work row of holes as follows: sl 1, * yo, k2tog, rep from * to last st, inc into last st. Change to larger needles and pattern:

Row 1: * K3, p1. Rep from * to last st, k1.
Row 2: P2, * k1, p3. Rep from * to last 3 sts, k1, p2.
Row 3: K1, * p1, k3. Rep from * to end.
Row 4: P2, * k1, p3. Rep from * to last 3 sts, k1, p2.

These 4 rows form the pattern. Cont in pattern until piece measures 14″ (36cm) from beg. End with right side facing.

Shape Armhole:
Cont in pattern and bind off 3 (3, 4, 5) sts at beg of next 2 rows. Then dec 1 st at each end of next and then every other row until 75 (75, 81, 81) sts. Cont in pattern until back measures 21½″ (54.5cm) from beg. End with right side facing.

Shape Shoulders:
Cont in pattern and bind off 11 (11, 12, 12) sts at beg of next 4 rows. Place rem 31 (31, 33, 33) sts onto holder for neckband.

Right Front:
With smaller needles, cast on 48 (50, 52, 55) sts and work as follows:
Row 1: Sl 1, k6, rib to end.
Row 2: Sl 1, rib to last 7 sts, k6, k1 tbl.
Repeat these 2 rows once more.
Row 5: Sl 1, k2, yo, k2 tog, k2 (buttonhole) rib to end. Cont in single rib and garter st border until piece measures 4″ (10cm), making buttonholes 14 rows apart (buttonholes continue up front band). On last row of ribbing, work row of holes as for back. Change to larger needles and work in pattern with garter st border as follows:

Row 1: Sl 1, k6, k24 (26, 24, 23), (k3, p1) 4 (4, 5, 6) times, k1.
Row 2 and all wrong side rows: P2, (k1, p3) 4 (4, 5, 6) times, purl to last 7 sts, k6, k1 tbl.
Row 3: Sl 1, k6, k2, MB, k21 (23, 21, 20), k1, (p1, k3) 4 (4, 5, 6) times.
Row 5: Sl 1, k6, k4, MB, k19 (21,19,18), (k3,p1) 4 (4, 5, 6) times, k1.
Row 7: Sl 1, k6, k2, MB, k3, MB, k17 (19, 17, 16), k1, (p1, k3) 4 (4, 5, 6) times.
Row 9: Sl 1, k6, k8, MB, k15 (17, 15, 14), (k3, p1) 4 (4, 5, 6) times, k1.
Row 11: Sl 1, k6, k2, MB, k7, MB, k13 (15, 13, 12), k1, (p1, k3) 4 (4, 5, 6) times.
Row 13: Sl 1, k6, k5, MB, k6, MB, k3, MB, k7 (9, 7, 6), (k3, p1) 4 (4, 5, 6) times, k1.

(NOTE: Work buttonhole every 14th row.)
Row 15: Work as for row 11.
Row 17: Work as for row 9.
Row 19: Work as for row 7.
Row 21: Work as for row 5.
Row 23: Work as for row 3.
Row 24: Work as for row 2.
These 24 rows form the pattern. Cont in pattern until piece measures 14″ (36cm) from beg. End with wrong side facing.

Shape Armhole:
Cont working in pattern and garter st border and bind off 3 (3, 4, 5) sts at beg of next row. Work 1 row. Dec 1 st at armhole edge on next and every other row until 41 (41, 44, 42) sts rem. Work evenly until

T YROL T REASURE

piece measures 18″ (46cm) from beg. End with right side facing. Pattern 15 sts then place on a holder for neckband, pattern to end of row. When 24th row of pattern is complete work bobble sts in st st and cont with broken rib pattern. Dec 1 st at neck edge on next row and then every other row until 22 (22, 24, 24) sts rem. Work evenly until front measures same as back to shoulder. End at side edge.

Shape Shoulder:
Bind off 11 (11, 12, 12) sts at beg of next row, then every other row once.

Left Front:
Work to match right front, reversing all shaping and omitting buttonholes. Pattern row will now read:

Row 1: Sl 1, (p1, k3) 4 (4, 5, 6) times, k24 (26, 24, 23), k6, k1 tbl.
Row 2: Sl 1, k6, purl to last 18 (18, 22, 26) sts, (p3, k1) 4 (4, 5, 6) times, p2.
Row 3: Sl 1, (k3, p1) 4 (4, 5, 6) times, k1, k21 (23, 21, 20), MB, k2, k6, k1 tbl.

Sleeves:
With smaller needles, cast on 39 (39, 41, 41) sts and work in k1, p1 rib for 3½″ (9cm). Inc 2 (2, 4, 4) sts across last row, 41 (41, 45, 45) sts. Change to larger needles and work in pattern as for back. Inc 1 st at each end of 5th row and then every 6th row until there are 67 (67, 71, 71) sts. Work evenly until piece measures 17½ (17½, 17½, 18)″ / 44.5 (44.5, 44.5, 46)cm from beg. End with right side facing.

Shape Cap:
Cont in pattern, bind off 3 sts at beg of next 4 rows, then dec 1 st at each end of every row until 45 (45, 49, 49) sts rem. Then dec 1 st at each end every other row until 35 (35, 39, 39) sts rem. Now dec 1 st each end every 3rd row until 23 sts rem. Bind off 4 sts at beg of next 4 rows. Bind off rem sts.

Neckband:
Sew shoulder seams. With smaller needles and right side facing, pick up 30 sts from right front, including 15 from holder, 31 (31, 33, 33) sts across back, and 30 sts down left front including 15 sts from holder. Work 3 rows in garter st. Inc 10 sts evenly across first row. Work 1 row of holes, as for back. Then work 4 rows of garter st. Bind off as follows: Bind off 2 sts, * sl st onto left hand needle, cast on 2 sts, bind off 4 sts. Rep from * to end.

Finishing:
Set sleeves into armholes and sew into place. Sew sleeve and side seams. Make 2 crochet chains in chain st one 30″ (76cm) long for neck; and one 40″ (102cm) for waist. The chains are threaded through holes. Finish chains with small neat tassels. Sew on buttons to match buttonholes.

Embroidery:
Embroidery is optional. Flowers are embroidered on with chain st petals and satin st centers, using sportweight yarn.

CLASSIC CRICKET

I feel every collection of handknits should include a good old cable sports sweater. In white with Club Colors, I call it a "Cricket" sweater. It's also super in any other color with the stripe interest to suit the individual.

■

Sizes:
To fit small, medium and large. Finished bust measurements 40 (42, 44)" / 102 (106, 112)cm. Directions are for small with larger sizes in parentheses.

Materials:
15 (16, 17) 50 gm balls of sportweight cotton in MC
1 50 gm ball of each CC (A & B)

Needles:
One pair each size 3 (3.25mm) and size 5 (4mm) knitting needles, or size needed to obtain gauge.

Gauge:
11 sts = 2" on #5 needles over st st.

Back:
With smaller needles and MC, cast on 106 (110, 114) sts and work in k1, p1 rib in stripe pattern as follows: 2 rows MC, 4 rows A, 4 rows B, 2 rows MC, 4 rows A, 4 rows B, 4 rows MC inc 10 sts evenly spaced across last row, 116 (120, 124) sts. Change to larger needles and work in rib and cable pattern as follows:

Row 1: Sl 1, k5 (7, 9), (p2, k12, p2, k6) 4 times, p2, k12, p2, k5 (7, 9), k1 tbl.
Row 2: Sl 1, p5 (7, 9), k2, p12, k2 (p6, k2, p12, k2) 4 times, k5 (7,9), k1 tbl.

Repeat these two rows 4 times more.

Row 11: Sl 1, k5 (7, 9), (p2, C6 [C6 = Cable 6 = Sl next 6 sts onto a cable needle and hold at back of work, k6, k6 from cable needle], p2, k6) 4 times, p2, C6, p2, k5 (7, 9), k1, tbl.
Row 12: Work as for row 2.
Rows 13–22: Repeat rows 1 and 2—5 times.

These 22 rows form the cable and rib pattern. Repeat these 22 rows twice (3 times, 3 times) more, then rows 1–16 once.

Shape Armholes:
Bind off 6 sts at beg of next 2 rows. Work evenly on cable and rib pattern until back measures 10½" (26.5cm) from start of armhole shaping. End right side facing.

Shape Shoulders:
Bind off 24 (27, 29) sts at beg of next 2 rows. (NOTE: K2 sts tog across 12 cable sts, which means you are actually binding off 36 (39, 41) sts. Place rem 32 (30, 30) on a holder for neck.

Front:
Work as for back to armhole shaping.

Shape Armhole & Front 'V' Shaping:
Bind off 6 sts. Pattern across 52 (54, 56) sts, turn, p2tog and pattern across. Cont in pattern and k2tog at neck edge next row and then every 3rd row until there are 36 (39, 41) sts. Work evenly until front measures same as back to shoulder. End with wrong side facing. Bind off, knitting 2 sts tog across the cables. Join yarn to other side and work to match first side, reversing all shaping.

Sleeves:
With smaller needles and MC, cast on 44 sts and work in k1, p1 rib in stripe pattern as for back. Inc 10 sts evenly spaced across last row, 54 sts. Change to larger needles and work in pattern as follows: Sl 1, k2, p2, k6, p2, k6, p2, k12, p2, k6, p2, k6, p2, k2, k1 tbl. Work as for pattern on body by cabling on 11th and every 22nd row, *at the same time,* inc 1 st at each end of 5th and then every 6th row until there are 100 sts (work extra sts in the k6, p2 rib). Work evenly until sleeve measures 20" (51cm) from beg.

Shape Cap:
Bind off 6 sts at beg of next 2 rows. Dec 1 st each end every row 19 times, 50 sts. Bind off on wrong side, knitting 2 sts tog across cables.

Neckband:
Sew right shoulder seam. With smaller needles and MC, pick up 64 sts down left side, 1 st from center (mark this st), 64 sts up right side, and 32 (30, 30) sts from back. Work in k1, p1 rib in stripe pattern, knitting 3 center sts tog every row. Stripe pattern: 1 row MC, 4 rows A, 4 rows B, 1 row MC. Then bind off in MC, knitting 3 center front sts tog.

Finishing:
Sew in ends. Sew left shoulder seam. Sew in sleeves and sew up sleeve and side seams.

Sleeveless Version:
10 50 gm balls of sportweight cotton MC
1 50 gm ball of each CC

Work back and front as for long sleeved sweater. Join left shoulder seam. Pick up and work neckband the same as long sleeved version. Join right shoulder seam.

Armbands:
With smaller needles and MC, with right side facing pick up 120 sts around armhole. Work in k1, p1 rib in stripe pattern as follows: 1 row MC, 2 rows A, 2 rows B, 1 row MC. Bind off in rib.

Join side seams.

Ming Vase

Flower patterns are a permanent part of fashion and this charming little camisole is a floral design with a difference. Although I have mostly made it in a cream base with differing depths of color for the flowers, it also looks great using heathery or soft pastels or neutrals for the base. A lovely summer garment.

Sizes:
One size fits all. Finished measurement 38" (96cm).

Materials:
7 50 gm balls sportweight cotton in cream (MC)
1 50 gm ball each of coral, pink, green
small amounts of aqua and mauve

Needles:
One pair of each size 1 (2.5mm) and size 4 (3.5mm), or size needed to obtain gauge.

Gauge:
11 sts = 2" (5cm) on #4 needles worked over st st.

Front:
With smaller needles and MC, cast on 110 sts and work in k1, p1 rib and Tree of Life pattern (see A Summer Sculpture), until piece measures 2½" (6cm) from beg. Change to larger needles and follow chart to end of 90th row.

Shape Armholes:
Cont to follow pattern and bind off 6 sts at beg of next 2 rows. Then dec 1 st at beg of the next 12 rows, 86 sts. Cont up chart to end of 114th row.

Shape Neck:
Pattern across 25 sts, turn, and work this side only. Dec 1 st at neck edge every other row until 11 sts rem. Work evenly in MC when pattern is complete. When piece measures 22½" (57cm) from beg, end wrong side facing. Bind off in k st. Join yarn to rem sts, bind off center 36 sts and work second side to correspond to first, reversing all shaping.

Back:
Work rib as for front, but *decrease* 6 sts evenly across last row, 104 sts. Change to larger needles and work in st st until back is the same length as front to armholes.

Shape Armholes:
Bind off 4 sts at beg of next 2 rows. Then dec 1 st at beg of next 10 rows, 86 sts. Work evenly until back measures 17½" (44.5cm) from beg. End with right side facing. Follow back chart to end of 15th row.

Shape Neck:
Pattern across chart for 27 sts, turn and work this side only. Dec 1 st at neck edge on every row until 11 sts rem. Work in MC only until same length as front to shoulder. End with wrong side facing. Bind off in k st.

Join yarn to rem st, bind off 32 sts and work second side to match first, reversing all shaping.

Finishing:
Sew shoulder and side seams. Work one or two rows of single crochet around the neck and armholes.

MING VASE

□ = Cream—Main Color
× = Pink
▼ = Green
● = Coral
○ = Coral
▽ = Aqua
\ = Mauve
◢ = Cream (Main)

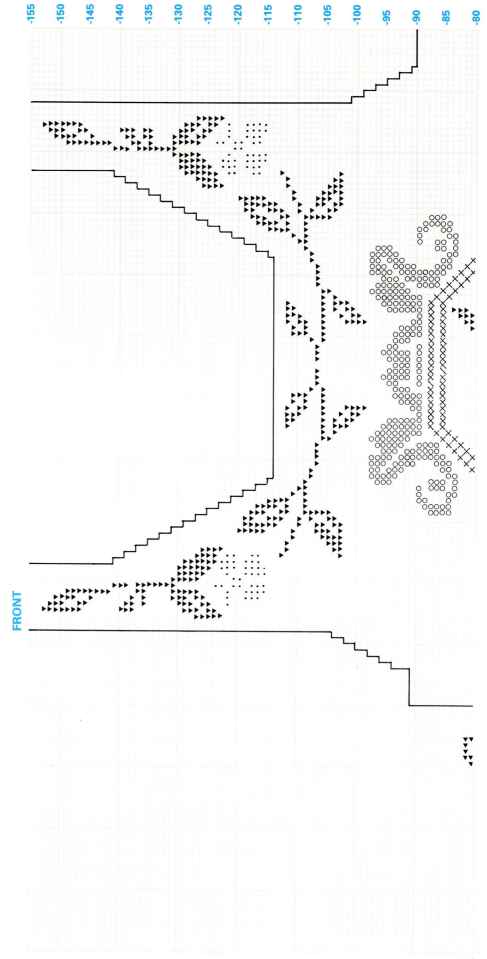

BACK

START THIS CHART WHEN
BACK MEASURES 17½"

LACY DAYS

A very special vest knitted in a lace design with paisley motifs formed by bobbles on seed stitch or seed stitch alone. Its delicacy will enhance any outfit from the most casual to the most exotic.

Sizes:
To fit up to 34 (38)″ / 86 (96)cm bust. Directions are for small with medium in parentheses.

Materials:
5 50 gm balls of fingering weight mercerised cotton
6 small buttons

Needles:
One pair each size 1 (2.5mm) and size 2 (3mm) knitting needles, or size needed to obtain gauge.

Gauge:
17 sts = 2″ (5cm) over st st on #2 (3mm) needles

Note:
This lace garment is knitted with a simple lace stitch used for the background with single seed stitch motifs with bobbles knitted into the background stitch. The motifs are charted thus:

Square marked with X = seed stitch
● = bobbles

The lace stitch is a simple multiple of 2 and a single row pattern. All rows = *yo, p2tog, rep from * across row. (yo = yarn around needle). Each row begins with sl 1, k1 tbl and ends with k1, k1 tbl to give a firm edge to lace. Bobbles = (p1, k1, p1) into st, turn k3, turn p3, pass 2nd and 3rd st over 1st st. Bobbles are always made on right side rows.

Left Front:
With larger needles cast on 4 sts and work as follows:

Row 1: Sl 1, p2, k1 tbl, cast on 2 sts.
Row 2: (wrong side) K2 tbl, yo, p2tog, k1, k1 tbl, cast on 2 sts.
Row 3: K2 tbl, (yo, p2tog) twice, k1, k1 tbl, cast on 2 sts.
Row 4: K2 tbl, (yo, p2tog) 3 times, k1, k1 tbl, cast on 2 sts.

Cont in pattern, casting on 2 sts at end of every row, and working (yo, p2tog) an extra time every row. *At the same time* beg following chart. When there are 52 (60) sts work evenly, following chart, until armhole shaping. End with right side facing.

Shape Armhole:
Bind off 6 sts at armhole edge, then 2 sts every other row (armhole edge) twice. Work 1 row.

Shape Neck:
Next row dec 2 sts at neck edge, then every 8th row 9 times, 22 (30) sts. Cont in lace st until piece measures 19″ (48cm) from beg. With wrong side facing bind off in k st.

Right Front:
Work as for left front, reversing all shaping. (Follow chart for pattern and dec.)

Back:
With smaller needles cast on 116 (132) sts and work in k1, p1 rib for 8 rows. On last row inc 29 sts evenly spaced across row, 145 (161) sts. Change to larger needles and work in st st until back measures same as front (do not measure points) to armhole. End with right side facing.

Shape Armholes:
Bind off 12 sts at the beg of the next 2 rows, then dec 1 st at each end of next and then every other row 10 times. Work evenly until back measures same as front to shoulder. End with right side facing.

Shape Shoulders:
Bind off 25 (33) sts at beg of next 2 rows. Bind off rem sts.

Finishing:
Sew side and sleeve seams. Beg at right side, single crochet down right point, up point, up right front, around neck, down left front, down left point and up left point. Fasten off.
Sew buttons into place. Crochet chain st loop to fit buttons. Single crochet around armholes.

LACY DAYS

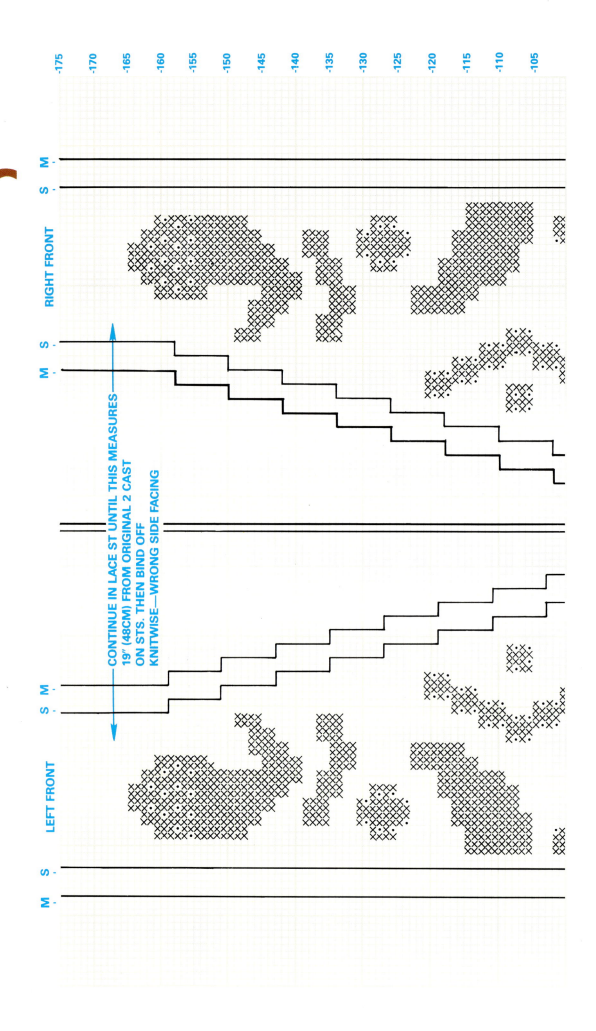

CONTINUE IN LACE ST UNTIL THIS MEASURES 19" (48CM) FROM ORIGINAL 2 CAST ON STS. THEN BIND OFF KNITWISE—WRONG SIDE FACING

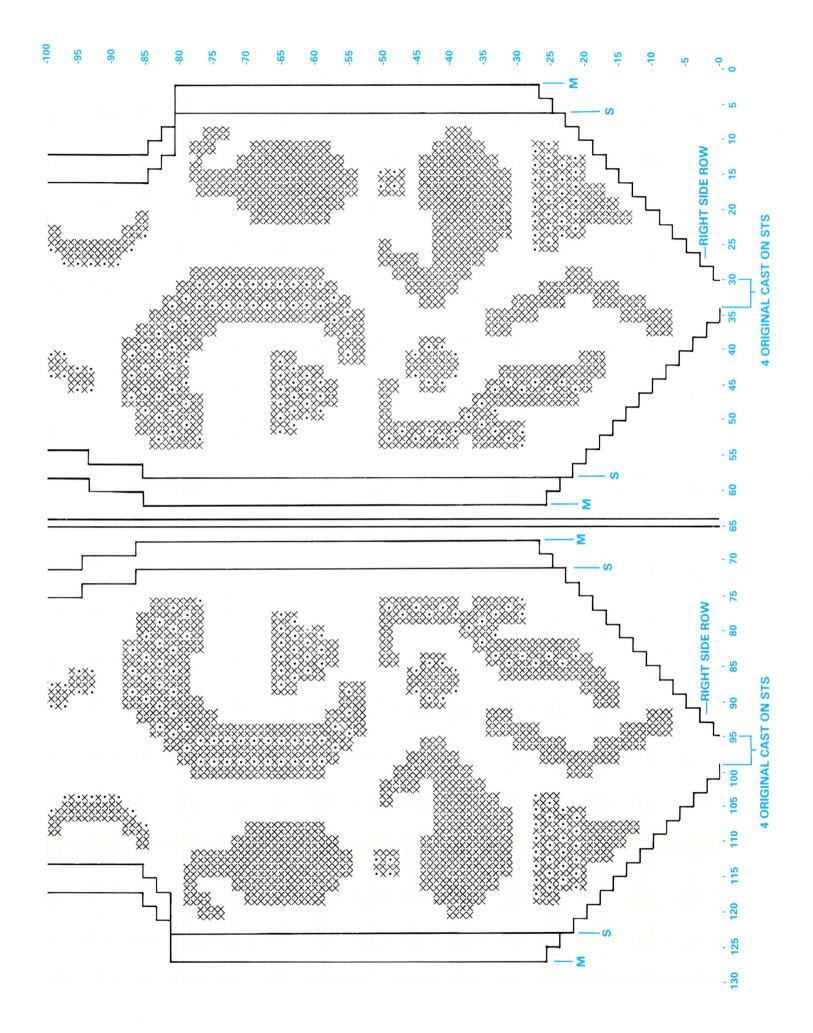

Summer-Time Blues

I'm very proud of this design. It takes a long time to make because it has to be knitted on very small needles. However, it is more than worth the effort to create this variety of delicate and old fashioned stitches. I think it is one of the most beautiful handknits in the world, a real collector's item. Incidentally, it washes beautifully.

Sizes:
One size, fits up to 36″ (96cm) bust. Finished measurement 39″ (99cm).

Materials:
8 50 gm balls of fingering weight cotton yarn
3 buttons

Needles:
One pair each size 1 (2.5mm) and size 2 (3mm) knitting needles. Or size needed to obtain gauge.

Gauge:
16 sts = 2″ on #2 needles in st st.

Back:
With smaller needles, cast on 117 sts and work in k1, p1 rib for 3″ (7.5cm). Inc in every 3rd st across last row, 156 sts. Change to larger needles and work as follows:

Row 1: Knit
Row 2: Purl
Row 3: K1 * yo, k2tog. Rep from * to end, k1.
Row 4: Knit

These 4 rows form the first row of holes which act as dividing lines (vertically and horizontally) between the squares.

Row 5: Sl 1, yo, k2tog, work across 35 sts of 1st row of sampler #5, k1, yo, k2tog, work across 36 sts of 1st row of sampler #4, k1, yo, k2tog, work across 35 sts of 1st row of sampler #2, k1, yo, k2tog, work across 35 sts of 1st row of sampler #1, k1, yo, k2tog.
Row 6: K3, pattern across 2nd row of #1, k3, pattern across 2nd row of #2, k3, pattern across 2nd row of #4, k3, pattern across 2nd row of #5, k3.
Row 7: As 5th, but working across 3rd row of each square instead of first.

Cont in this way with holes dividing squares for 48 rows, 3½″ (9cm). Then work rows 1 through 4 to make dividing row of holes. (NOTE: Some of the sampler squares need 36 sts instead of 35. The odd stitch must be made on the first row of such a square and dec on the last row within the square. The dividing line of holes must be kept straight.)

Next row: Work as for 5th row, working across samplers #6, #3, #7 and #8. Work the 48 rows of these squares still divided by holes.

Work rows 1 through 4 to make dividing row of holes. Work as for 5th row, setting samplers #9, #10, #11, and #5. Work the 48 rows. Work rows 1 through 4 to make dividing row of holes. Work as for 5th row, setting samplers #11, #9, #6, and #1. Work the 48 rows.

Shape Shoulders:
Bind off 16 sts at beg of the next 6 rows. Place rem 60 sts on holder for neckband.

Front:
Work as for back until 5th row in last set of samplers (24 rows have been worked).

Shape Neck:
Next row: Work across 60 sts and turn. Dec 1 st at neck edge on every row, until 48 sts rem. Work evenly until squares are complete. End at side edge.

Shape Shoulders:
Bind off 16 sts at beg of next row and then every other row twice more. Return to rem sts and sl center 36 onto holder for neckband. Work to match first side, reversing all shaping.

Sleeves:
With smaller needles, cast on 50 sts and work in k1, p1 rib for 3″ (7.5cm). Inc into every st on last row, 100 sts. Change to larger needles and work granite ridges (follow sampler #9). Inc 1 st at each end of 13th and then every 10th row until there are 136 sts. Work evenly until piece measures 18″ (46cm) from beg. End with wrong side facing. Bind off.

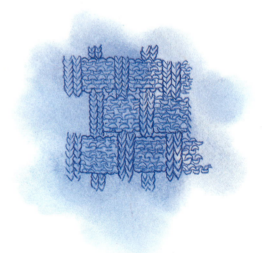

SUMMER-TIME BLUES

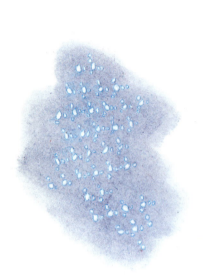

Neckband:
Sew right shoulder seam. With smaller needles and right side facing, pick up 25 sts down left front, 36 sts from center front, 25 sts up right front and 60 sts from back. Work in k1, p1 rib for 5 rows. Bind off in rib.

Finishing:
Sew left shoulder seam, leaving 2½" (6cm) open at neck edge. Sew sleeves into place by matching center sleeves to shoulder seam. Sew side and sleeve seams. Sew three buttons into place. Crochet chain st loops to fit buttons.

The Sampler Squares

SAMPLER NO. 1 Across 35 sts × 3½" (9cm).
Row 1: knit.
Row 2: purl.
Row 3: * k5, k2tog, M1, k1, M1, sl 1, k1, psso. Rep from * twice, k5.
Row 4: p5, * p2, sl 1 purlwise, p7. Rep from * twice.
Row 5: As 3rd.
Row 6: As 4th.
Row 7: knit.
Row 8: purl.
Row 9: *k2tog, M1, k1, M1, sl 1, k1, psso, k5, Rep from * twice, k2tog, M1, k1, M1, k1.
Row 10: * p2, sl 1 purlwise, p7. Rep from * twice, p2, sl 1 purlwise, p2.
Row 11: As 9th.
Row 12: As 10th.

Repeat these twelve rows for 3½" (9cm).

SAMPLER NO. 2 Across 35 sts × 3½" (9cm).
Row 1: k16, p3, k6.
Row 2: p16, k3, p16.
Row 3: k15, p5, k15.
Row 4: p15, k5, p15.
Row 5: k14, p3, k1, p3, k14.
Row 6: p14, k3, p1, k3, p14.
Row 7: k13, p3, k3, p3, k13.
Row 8: p13, k3, p3, k3, p13.
Row 9: k12, p3, k5, p3, k12.
Row 10: p12, k3, p5, k3, p12.
Row 11: k11, p3, k3, p1, k3, p3, k11.
Row 12: p11, k3, p3, k1, p3, k3, p11.

Continue sloping in this way until 3½" (9cm) has been worked.

SAMPLER NO. 3 Across 36 sts × 3½" (9cm) (Broken Chevron)
Row 1: * k1, p2, k2, p2, k1, p1. Rep from * to end.
Row 2: * k3, p2, k2, p2, k1, (p2, k2) twice. Rep from * once.
Row 3: * p1, k2, p2, k2, p3, (k2, p2) twice. Rep from * once.
Row 4: * k1, p2, k2, p2, k5, p2, k2, p2.

Rep from * once.
Rep these 4 rows for 3½" (9cm).

SAMPLER NO. 4 Across 36 sts × 3½" (9cm) (Double Seed)
Row 1: * k2, p2. Rep from * to end.
Row 2: As 1st.
Row 3: * p2, k2. Rep from * to end.
Row 4: As 3rd.

Rep these 4 rows for 3½" (9cm).

SAMPLER NO. 5 Across 35 sts × 3½" (9cm) (Fancy Trellis)
Row 1: * k2, k2tog, yo, k3. Rep from * to end.
Row 2: * p1, p2tog tbl, yo, p1, yo, p2tog, p1. Rep from * to end.
Row 3: * k2tog, yo, k3, yo, sl 1, k1, psso. Rep from * to end.
Row 4: purl.
Row 5: * yo, sl 1, k1, psso, k5. Rep from * to end.
Row 6: * yo, p2tog, p2, p2tog tbl, yo, p1. Rep from * to end.
Row 7: * k2, yo, sl 1, k1, psso, k2tog, yo, k1. Rep from * to end.
Row 8: purl.

Rep these 8 rows for 3½" (9cm).

SAMPLER NO. 6   Across 36 sts × 3½″ (9cm) (Knot St)
Row 1: knit.
Row 2: purl.
Row 3: knit.
Row 4: purl.
Row 5: k3, MK. Rep from * to end. (MK = make knot = p3tog, leave st on left hand needle, yo, p tog same 3 sts—still 3 sts).
Row 6: purl.
Row 7: knit.
Row 8: purl.
Row 9: knit.
Row 10: purl.
Row 11: * MK, k3. Rep from * to end.
Row 12: purl.

Rep these 12 rows for 3½″ (9cm).

SAMPLER NO. 7   Across 36 sts × 3½″ (9cm) (Shooting Star)
Row 1: k1, k3, k2tog, k4, yo, p2 (k2, yo, sl 1, k1, psso), 3 times, p2, yo, k4, sl 1, k1, psso, k3, k1.
Row 2: k1, p2, p2tog tbl, p4, yo, p1, k2, (p2, yo, p2tog) 3 times, k2, p1, yo, p4, p2tog, p2, k1.
Row 3: k1, k1, k2tog, k4, yo, k2, p2, (k2, yo, sl 1, k1, psso) 3 times, p2, k2, yo, k4, sl 1, k1, psso, k2.
Row 4: k1, p2tog tbl, p4, yo, p3, k2, (p2, yo, p2tog) 3 times, k2, p3, yo, p4, p2tog, k1.
Rows 5–12: Repeat rows 1–4 twice more.
Row 13: k1, yo, sl 1, k1, psso, k2, yo, sl 1, k1, psso, p2, yo, k4, sl 1, k1, psso, k6, k2tog, k4, yo, p2, k2, yo, sl 1, k1, psso, k3.
Row 14: k1, yo, p2tog, p2, yo, p2tog, k2, p1, yo, p4, p2tog, p4, p2tog tbl, p4, yo, p1, k2, p2, yo, p2tog, p2, k1.
Row 15: k1, yo, sl 1, k1, psso, k2, yo, sl 1, k1, psso, p2, k2, yo, k4, sl 1, k1, psso, k2, k2tog, k4, yo, k2, p2, k2, yo, sl 1, k1, psso, k3, k1.
Row 16: k1, yo, p2tog, p2, yo, p2tog, k2, p3, yo, p4, p2tog, p2 tbl, p4, yo, p3, k2, p2, yo, p2tog, p2, k1.
Rows 17–24: Repeat rows 13–16 twice more.

Rep these 24 rows for 3½″ (9cm).

SAMPLER NO. 8   Across 36 sts × 3½″ (9cm) (Basket St)
Row 1: knit.
Row 2: purl.
Row 3: * k1, p4, k1. Rep from * to end.
Row 4: * p1, k4, p1. Rep from * to end.
Row 5: As 3rd.
Row 6: As 4th.
Row 7: knit.
Row 8: purl.
Row 9: * p2, k2, p2. Rep from * to end.
Row 10: * k2, p2, k2. Rep from * to end.
Row 11: As 9th.
Row 12: As 10th.

Rep these 12 rows for 3½″ (9cm).

SAMPLER NO. 9   Across 36 sts × 3½″ (9cm) (Granite Ridges)
Row 1: knit.
Row 2: purl.
Row 3: knit.
Row 4: purl.
Row 5: knit.
Row 6: k2tog all along row.
Row 7: (k1, p1) into every st.
Row 8: purl.

Rep these 8 rows for 3½″ (9cm).

SAMPLER NO. 10   Across 35 sts × 3½″ (9cm) (Granite St)
Row 1: * k1, p1, k1, (yo, k2tog tbl) twice. Rep from * to end.
Row 2: * (M1, p2tog) twice, k1, p1, k1. Rep from * to end.

Rep these 2 rows for 3½″ (9cm).

SAMPLER NO. 11   Across 35 sts × 3½″ (9cm).
Row 1: * k2, p2tog, yo, k1. Rep from * to end.
Rows 2, 4, 6, 8: purl.
Row 3: knit.
Row 5: * k3, yo, p2tog. Rep from * to end.
Row 7: knit.

Rep these 8 rows for 3½″ (9cm).

ABOUT THE DESIGNER

Nancy Vale is an ordinary English mum
who has been knitting and designing
extraordinary sweaters for most of her life.
A fanatic knitter since she was eight years
old, Nancy combined her love of knitting
with her love for children to found Nancy
Vale of London Ltd., producers of fine
baby knitwear. Over the years, Nancy's
talents have focused on high fashion
knitwear, and her company is now a
renowned resource for couture houses and
specialty stores all over the world. Nancy
has 1000 knitters throughout Britain who
create the garments which are distributed
through her headquarters in Welling,
Kent, and she has published a series of
magazines of her designs.
Nancy has five children and makes her
home in Kent.

PHOTO AND ILLUSTRATION CREDITS

Illustrations by Marika Hahn

Charts by Bill Meyerriecks

Photographs on pages ii, 2–3, 25, 28–29, 45, 53, 69, 70–71, 85, 110–11, and 137 by Stephen Aucoin; styling by Gail Sadow
Photographs on pages 5, 31, and 37 by Martin Brading
Photographs on pages 9, 11, 17, 21, 41, 49, 59, 63, 65, 73, 75, 79, 91, 95, 101, 103, 119, 129, 131, 135, and 145 by Chris Grout-Smith
Photographs on pages 13, 67, and 109 by Victor Yuan
Photographs on pages 113, 123, 125, and 141 by Dave Anthony
The following generously provided clothing and accessories for the photographs by Stephen Aucoin: Back in Black, Bettina Riedel, Carlos Falchi, Central Carpet, Cole Hahn, Gene Ewing for Bis, Harriet Selwyn at Madison Avenue Design Group, Jewel Case, Laura Ashley, Locomotive, Jaeger, Marla Buck, Maude Frizon, Optic Zone, Patricia Underwood, Robert Underwood-Natural Comfort-Madison Avenue, Ron Chereskin, Sentimento, Tahari, UBU, Vittorio Ricci. Thanks also to Chez Ma Tante Restaurant, NYC, and the Millbrook Golf and Country Club, Millbrook, New York.